A
KINSHIP
Guide to
Rescuing Children

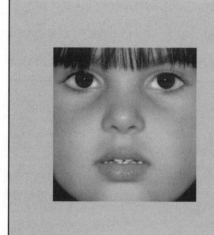

for
Grandparents
and
Other Relatives
as Parents

Helene LaBrecque Ellis

A Kinship Guide to Rescuing Children
for Grandparents and Other Relatives as Parents

Copyright 2008 Helene Ellis
Published by Chicago Road Publishing LLC
Post Office Box 1073
Okemos, Michigan 48805

Editor: Helene Ellis

Book design: Lisa Sullivan, lisadsullivan@comcast.net

Cover: Photographer – ©Marilyn Barbone - Fotolia.com

The information in this book, *A Kinship Guide to Rescuing Children*, is for informational purposes only. The resources noted in the text and in the Resources section are intended to be a guide to some of the possible sources available to kinship care providers. Chicago Road Publishing and Helene Ellis are not responsible for the content of the resources suggested including any advertisements for goods or services. Suggestions for advocacy or outreach are just that – suggestions – to help kinship care providers recognize the choices available to them in the course of action that they may want to take.

Nothing in this guide should be construed as legal or therapeutic advice or counseling. The information provided is not a substitute for consulting with an experienced family law attorney or qualified family counselor or therapist based on the facts and circumstances of each particular kinship care situation.

ISBN-13: 978-0-9801352-0-6
ISBN-10: 0980135206

Printed in the United States of America
Book manufactured by Thomson-Shore, Dexter Michigan

Acknowledgements

This book has been years in the making. Over that time, hundreds of families willingly shared their hard and sometimes funny stories on raising the children from extended family. The names of all these good folks cannot be included here, but they know who they are and now I hope they know that they are the first acknowledgement toward the production of this work. From there we have many people who contributed to this guidebook.

Thank you to the good people of Hillsdale County, Michigan who diligently work hard at their professional jobs and with their families to secure the health of the whole community. Thank you to the various services dedicated to the children in the State of Michigan. Though this book has tried to incorporate services to families across the nation, I also relied on exceptional sources in my home state. Beautiful Michigan is where I learned to understand the processes that make children's services happen. I am grateful to those who bravely face the challenges of this important work every day.

Specifically, *A Kinship Guide to Rescuing Children*, offers thank you to some very special individuals: Terry Vear, Executive Director of Hillsdale County Senior Services Center for allowing me the freedom to create a full service Kinship Care Program so many years ago. Thank you to Jane Sanderson who carried on and kept opening doors for me as the work on the book progressed. Thank you to professional advisors – Joe Kozakiewicz, Director, MSU Chance at Childhood Program; Steven Murphy for reviews of the social services system; Chris Bishop, IS Coordinator; Marsha Kreucher, CEO Community Action Agency; Ama Agyemang, Program Coordinator Kinship Care Resource Center, Michigan; Leon LaBrecque, CEO LJPR, LLC for keeping me on track with finances; Thomas S. Condon,

CPA; Jessie Ellis, editorial advice; Jordan Brittany Ellis, for extensive typing work; Gary L. Bender, attorney, Murphy, Brenton & Spagnuolo, P.C.; Lisa Sullivan, typesetter, for excellent advice and especially gentle patience with me. Moral support from my agent, Evelyn Fazio; Edward James Olmos who graciously called me personally to offer good wishes with the project; John Weise, for marketing advice; Ah-ha information from Elizabeth Sullivan; James Brosseau; Miriam Bender, Liz Weise. Most grateful thanks to Tamara LaBrecque (Mom) for constant encouragement and wisdom, for being my angel; my wonderful children and grandchildren who enrich my thoughts every hour of every day; and a special acknowledgement to Joel Ellis, my husband, without whom I could not have even tackled a project of this size.

To see their names there, simple in 11 point type, just doesn't seem enough. I am so grateful to all of you, not only for the work on this guidebook, but for the good work that all of you do. You are truly my heroes.

Table of Contents

Acknowledgements... *i*
Welcome.. *iv*

Section I:
How Did This Happen?
  Getting Organized... 1
  Becoming a Kinship Care Provider (Legal Options)......... 9
  The Trip to Social Services.. 31
  Other Community Services... 45
  When to Seek Counseling.. 53
  School: A Child's Full Time Job.................................... 71
  Child Care Considerations... 85

Section II:
The Long Term Commitment
  Financial Planning (Get a Will, Money for the Future)..... 93
  Children and Money.. 107
  Children in Today's Electronic World............................ 113
  Finding Resources (Computer Basics)........................... 127
  Don't Forget to Have Fun.. 139

Section III:
The Community Kinship Care Resource Center
  Types of Community Kinship Care Support Programs.... 147
  Establishing a *Comprehensive* Kinship Care Program........ 155

Section IV:
Resources. Resources. Resources.
  Resources by Topic... 181
  State Departments of Health and Human Services.......... 197
  State Contacts for Central Kinship Care........................ 203
  Books on Kinship Care.. 213
  States Census Chart.. 215

Welcome

Dear Reader – After years of working with families who have just taken on a beloved child (more likely children), I have learned that there are few resources guiding these courageous adults through the maze of public systems. This book is not about how to parent someone else's child. There are many excellent guides addressing specific psychological issues facing kinship care families. Rather, this book is a humble sharing of the many decisions caregivers may face with public systems after taking on the task of relative care.

Grandparents and other kinship care providers (aunts and uncles, brothers and sisters, Godparents) are very special and valued surrogate parents. They take on a terrific rescue at considerable cost to themselves, and provide a significant service to the society at large saving millions in child welfare dollars. Quietly kinship caregivers raise traumatized children providing safe, secure, loving homes. In the process they may seek services from resources that are often more frustrating than helpful. They pay for medical, dental, psychological help, support their charges in schools, sports, and friendships. All of this is done to launch a *healthy* young adult into the world.

First let's get the name issue out of the way. To name the special group of non-parent relatives who are raising related children has been a difficult task for all of us who work in the field. Many organizations began with *Grandparents Raising Grandchildren* because that population grew significantly in the 1980's and finally became counted in the U.S. Census of the last two decades. Then social service concerns recognized that many other non-parent relatives were raising children

What do we call these folks?

Well, we are still not settled. *Relative* is good in most cases, but then, parents are relatives too. So we stumble over more words. *Kin* and *Kinship care* could refer to adults caring for the elderly as well.

In spite of the desire to title this book with strong emotional words, I chose a title with as many "key" words to fit our fast-emerging electronic world of search engines. Forgive me for having such a mundane reason to such a special group of people. To shorten the title, the book will be referred to as *A Kinship Guide*. To avoid monotonous repetition, you will read many terms throughout the book referring to families – *relative caregivers, kinship care providers,* even *grandfamilies* which is my favorite because you are all truly grand-families.

Grandparents and other kinship caregivers receive very little acknowledgment for the effort involved in what is often an intense parenting experience. Grandparents who raise their grandchildren and other relatives who take on additional parenting roles are a treasure to our society.

What we, as a society, know about kinship care is skimpy and from scattered sources. We know the commonly repeated figure from the 2000 U.S. Census that 2.4 million grandparents and 1.5 million other non-parent relatives are raising over 6 million children. Keep in mind that Census figure is almost a decade old as of this writing. If the rate of increase from the previous two decades continues, by 2010, close to 4.5 million non-parent families will be raising related children.

Media visions of kinship care families have had some impact on the progress of services. If the general public even thinks about the issue of kinship care, the view is either that these are economically poor families or young hip singles rich enough to deal with the issues. The reality is that kinship care crosses all economic, ethnic, and geographic areas of our society.

When I speak to a non-kinship care group, several individuals will tell of someone they know that has cared for a related child. In today's world of changing generational lifestyles and values, more and more children and relatives are vulnerable to kinship care situations. When we stereotype various populations we deny ourselves important community discussions that could not only solve problems, but enrich us all. Facing the issues with kinship care families requires both a national and local view. In other words, rural families do struggle with serious economic issues including distance from public services. Tribal communities face specific issues of residence and ethnic identification. African-American families, both urban and rural, face the challenge of raising related children against other social obstacles. Other close knit cultures in our American society, such as some families with Latino or Asian roots, may prefer to keep kinship care issues silent from the world outside of their families which often complicates their ability to make authorized decisions for the children.

The ethnicity of these millions of grandfamilies is an issue only when, as a nation, we try to understand and appreciate various cultural values. The total of millions of relatives who have taken on the grand task of raising traumatized children reflect the sufferings of other difficulties in our society. Poverty, drugs, crimes are disproportioned within various geographic, parental age, or ethnic groups. These issues must be resolved, soon hopefully, in another public arena. It is the grandfamilies that catch the child when social ills strike. The problems experienced by all caregivers are very much the same – safety, food, shelter, health, time to love.

Relatives in this situation are burdened with a myriad of stressful concerns when they decide to accept the responsibility of raising a relative's child:

- money needs and often their own limited income
- children in need of special counseling services (there is a reason that children are not living with their parents)

- medical expenses for themselves and children that fall through the cracks of changing social structures.

Taking on the responsibility of care means entering into challenging public systems: schools, social services, legal institutions. At times these encounters are intimidating and exhausting for caregivers.

Grandparents may also suffer a specific spectrum of grief –

- Losing or at odds with their own adult child,
- Loss of treasured relationships with the siblings of their absent child,
- Loss of being a grandparent in that special way separate from the demands of parenting,
- Strains on their marriage, especially in second marriage stepfamilies,
- Loss of friends and long anticipated leisure time.

Grandparents often feel a sense of shame that they perceive as not raising their own children well. The shame sometimes appears as embarrassment to friends and community, especially if the adult child has committed a crime, abused or neglected their children, or suffers addictions that prevent them from caring for their children. In extreme cases where the adult child has been murdered, particularly by the other parent as a result of domestic violence, grandparents experience a terrible sense of grief that is tormented by guilt or shame. Unfortunately, care of the children in the aftermath of domestic violence murders is not uncommon.

About this Book

This is not a how-to-parent book. I wish I knew the secrets of successful parenting. My own children are wonderful adults who, like the rest of us, are burdened with a variety of social challenges. Even with a fully focused heart, I could not protect them from frustrated marriages or events of abuse outside our home. Instead, it has been in my work with hundreds of families that motivated the book you are reading.

The intent of *A Kinship Guide* is to provide a concise source of advocacy for relative caregivers who find themselves unexpectedly raising related children.

A Kinship Guide is divided into four main sections:

1. How Did This Happen – identifying individual situations, legal options, social services and other community services, counseling, schools, child care, and the endless organization of important papers.
2. The Long Term Commitment – get a Will, financial planning, children and money, children in an electronic world, finding resources.
3. Community Kinship Care Resource Center – what a strong local program can offer, how to start a kinship care program where none exists.
4. Resources, Resources, Resources.

The federal Department of Health and Human Services (DHHS) is the main body addressing the physical needs of families. State names for DHHS vary considerably. I often refer to this very important agency as *social services*.

Child Protective Services (CPS) refers to the department within the larger Department of Health and Human Services that deals with child welfare, abuse and neglect, child placement and foster care.

The Resources Section of the book attempts to provide the most recent names and contacts for human services departments by state. These, of course, will change but may provide a base to find the new resource. I have consulted experts in their fields for accuracy of the information in various sections, and tried to provide the most current information possible. The intention of *A Kinship Guide* is to help caregivers become advocates for their new families. Case stories told here have names and situations altered for obvious reasons. Though all are based on true situations, they have been fictionalized to support the chapter information. The value of these stories is to help readers recognize situations that may be helpful to them. Each chapter will have a story in italic print.

About the Author - Helene

My years of community service began with answering a call to organize a child abuse prevention program for a rural community in south central Michigan. The Social Services leaders and I in our community learned a great deal about the business of organizing – establishing a non-profit, working with a board of directors, fundraising, all the while staying focused to the job of trying to prevent the horrors of child abuse. As a result of that work I was asked by the Children's Trust Fund of Michigan to provide workshops on organizing for other communities around the State. I also had the opportunity to serve on the Board of Child Abuse Prevention for the state of Michigan.

In addition to working in Child Abuse Prevention services, I helped to develop and secure a viable Kinship Care Program for the local Senior Services Center which has provided services to hundreds of children and grandparents and other relatives since its inception. Every job builds on another, doesn't it. Both Child Abuse Prevention and Kinship Care Centers are organizations that do better when the whole community understands the issues and works together to improve the lives of families and so improving the whole community.

The next job for me fit right into my experiences on social programs working together: Coordinator for a collaborative body of two dozen human services organizations, legislative, and legal entities. Collaboration is a profound tool for strengthening individuals, families and whole communities.

The collaborative body that I worked for effectively and efficiently addressed the specific needs of kinship care and child abuse prevention by acting on the cross over needs such as housing, medical care and transportation. Imagine 24 diverse agencies with various missions and personalities all working together. I loved that job.

The work in these fields has been exhilarating and a gift of an unusual education. As far as I know there is no Social Work degree in Community Collaboration. I am so grateful for the opportunity of these experiences and especially to the families that greatly enriched my work life. Most importantly, I learned that there are heroes in our communities quietly doing the critical job of raising worried children.

Finally, as you, dear reader, find sections of *A Kinship Guide to Rescuing Children* that apply to your situation, please realize that though I do not know you personally, I know who you are and the tremendous task you have taken on. The kinship care providers that I have had the privilege to work with are the true givers of guidance throughout the production of this work. A sincere gratitude to all kinship care families is humbly acknowledged here. Thank you.

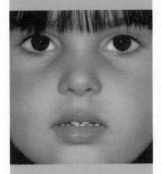

How Did This Happen?

Getting Organized

Becoming a Kinship Care Provider - Legal Options

The Trip to Social Services

Other Community Services

When to Seek Counseling

School: A Child's Full Time Job

Child Care Considerations

Getting Organized

Though the issues of legal decisions, going to social services, working with schools, and all the other big concerns are foremost on the minds of relative caregivers, little compares with the anxiety of a lost document or contact number in the moments before a critical appointment. We have put this chapter before all others because so much depends on the ability to find a piece of important information. For kinship care providers the usual disarray that accumulates in our daily lives can become a nightmare when critical decisions for children are being made.

Alva, a single grandmother caring for her grandson Sammy at the request of her daughter, Sammy's mother, learned just how important it was to have notes of her kinship care. Alva started innocently noting on a calendar the day Sammy was left with her. She noted phone calls to Sammy from his mother, expenses for doctor appointments, and pre-school events.

Weeks went by when Alva finally received the call that her daughter was not coming back. At Alva's insistence she and her daughter arranged to establish Alva as Guardian for Sammy. When the time came for guardianship proceedings, Alva was able to show dates of contact between Mom and Sammy, progress at school, and other important items. The log essentially showed how Sammy was thriving under his grandmother's care.

Simply stated, specific records of care or events presented in a court hearing can significantly impress a judge who must make the decisions on behalf of the child's well-being.

It is never too late to get organized.

If children are placed with relatives in an emergency situation, providers should make a written note of the event and any necessary contact numbers right away if possible. The notation should be put in a place where it can be retrieved easily. If, in the heat of the event, a recording was neglected, getting caught up by noting information later during calmer moments is better than an "oh well it's too late now". It is so easy for all of us to just postpone important business notes until we find ourselves in a situation where we wish we had done something more to smooth the path.

Following are the valuable basic tools that relative parents can use to get organized:

- The Log
- The Important Papers File
- The Contact Card
- The Family Calendar

The Log

The first very important step in getting organized is to **keep a dated log** of events in the first few weeks or months of caring for grandchildren. The log shows how much care the kinship family has provided, how much the cost has been, and events that may assist as evidence in returning a child to a safe parental environment, or retain a child in the safe care of grandparents or other kinship caregivers.

The log should note such items as:

- times of parental phone calls,
- money provided or money spent,
- medical appointments with names of providers and cost,
- social services appointments with names of workers, case numbers, telephone numbers,
- brief outcome notes (*Johnny is signed up for MI Child insurance*).

Such a log of events can be a wall calendar with notes on specific dates or it can be a notebook designated just for the recording of events <u>with each entry dated</u>, or the very organized provider can keep a cross reference of the log in both types – the calendar and a notebook.

The log is not a personal journal. The log should *not* include personal opinions about any parties involved – parents, in-laws, workers, public systems. If there is a need to blow off steam about situations, providers can start a personal journal somewhere else, a journal that may one day burn in a back yard campfire. Or caregivers can vent safely using any number of other methods like going for a walk, screaming into a pillow, sucking on a lemon slice, or whatever works. The Log of kinship care events must be clean of personal opinions. The Log document may be needed in court and you don't want it tainted by opinions that could change as the situations change.

Important Papers File

A folder file with separate compartments labeled can save precious time and anxiety especially if started early in the care of grandchildren. You may roll your eyes at the following list. Just finding these papers in normal, calm situations can be exasperating. To find them in the middle of the night during an emergency child drop off seems like a silly inclusion here. However, you will need some of these documents for any long term situation of raising children.

Check the list and try to get what you can as soon after the children are dropped off. If the parent does not have records, try to trace back to where services were provided so that you can get copies, such as doctor offices or medical clinics for immunization records, lawyers or courts for legal authority documents.

You will need written permission of the parents to obtain these records or some form of legal authority such as guardianship papers. As you will learn, grandparents who have taken on the honorable task of raising their grandchildren have no authority in the eyes of public institutions. For the journey ahead try to get any or all of the following into a well stocked important papers file. Who knows, you may be able to hand it back to a grateful parent in a few weeks or months.

- <u>Emergency medical care consent note</u> (which all caregivers should have regardless of how long the children will be with them – see the chapter on Legal Options)
- Other <u>legal authority papers</u> (guardianship or temporary custody orders from a social service agency that has placed the child in the relative's home)
- <u>Birth certificate</u> (the *official* birth certificate from the State in which the child was born, not the cute hospital certificate with the baby footprints)
- The <u>child's medical records</u> (records from doctors or clinics, immunizations, glasses or other vision records, hearing, or disabilities information that officially diagnose a physical problem with the child)
- <u>School records</u> with contact numbers; if the children will be attending a new school, try to obtain previous

school records, report cards, special education records, assessment tests; *note:* caregivers should keep a *separate* school file of children's work and school policies, events, etc (see the chapter on Working With Schools)

- Insurance cards or papers including Medicaid information
- Social services records with contacts (especially if parents were/are participating in any social service program)
- Social security cards (it is unlikely that these can be obtained from parents; if the stay is long term, caregivers can get the cards from the Social Security Administration – www.ssa.gov Call: **1.800.772.1213** between 7 a.m. – 7 p.m. TTY 1.800.325.0778
- Social security benefit records children who are receiving benefits because of parental disability or death will need to have access to the records.

Keeping the File Clean

As time goes by a number of other items will be added to this file that are specific to your family situation. Kinship families are unique in their need to be organized because situations change frequently. And, of course, every situation requires some valuable piece of paper somewhere in the file. Because of these changes, files should be cleaned periodically so that caregivers can avoid being overwhelmed looking for something important through a stack of papers with "old" and current items mixed together.

When cleaning the file, the group of papers most important to the current situation should be kept handy and filed by topic: medical, legal papers, etc.

The previously important papers, those not used in the current situation, should be put in an "Archive". These previously important papers may become important again sometime in the future. They should be placed in another part of the file folder identified as *archives*, or in large envelopes that are *labeled and dated* so that if you have to return to some of the papers you can access them easily.

Additional adequate storage of the important papers through the kinship care experience (which could be years) is not only a valuable resource when the cry for 'where-is" demands attention, it is also an historical record for your family.

Contact Card Information Source

In addition to an updated log and a well kept file folder of important papers, kinship caregivers may find keeping a card or pocket calendar with them in a purse or wallet with needed contact numbers becomes a valuable tool. The noted numbers might include the following:

- Social security numbers (for kin and child and maybe parent)
- Telephone numbers of services that are accessed often and names of contact persons (check this periodically as numbers change).
- Medicare, Medicaid and other social service cards or case numbers, including insurance account numbers and primary carriers.

In addition to a handy contact card, the easily accessible pocket calendar can be invaluable. There will be many appointments to note from doctor appointments to teacher conferences. The items can be transferred to the family calendar at home.

The PDA - Personal Digital Assistant. Kinship care providers who are electronically oriented and carry an electronic device that keeps track of the details of life, know the rules for use of these handy recording devices:

Back up everything and keep fresh batteries handy.

Life will be complicated enough with the addition of children without having to deal with lost information from the electronic data records.

The Family Calendar

Accessible for the whole family (separate from The Log). Where children's lives are involved and especially in kinship care where so many additional situations must be attended to, the Home Calendar becomes the main resource for organizing schedules – school activities, appointments, special events. A single source for all family members of these many events helps to keep everyone aware of what has happened and what is coming up. A home calendar keeps everyone on track.

Few of life's situations in today's world call for conscientious organizing like caring for a family member. The Log of the kinship care experience, a file folder with easily accessible categories for Important Papers, handy portable resources with contact numbers, and a one-stop family calendar posted in a visible spot for everyone to see can make life unbelievably easier for kinship care providers.

Getting organized and staying organized is an incredible tool in getting through the many situations relative caregivers need in order to launch a healthy young person into the world.

Becoming a
Kinship Care Provider

PART I:
How It All Happens

During a local kinship care meeting some folks introduced themselves by explaining how kinship care came about for them:

"My name is John. My wife and I are raising Elizabeth since her mother abandoned her and our son gave up parental rights to her. We got a lawyer and filed for a court order to become guardians."

"Hello – I'm Leila. My grandsons – Joseph and Ivan live with me. I am raising them like my grandmother raised me in Hungary. It's a family thing."

"I'm Maggie. And no one lives with me yet. I'm waiting for Social Services to transfer my little granddaughter, Eva, from Foster Care in Tennessee. I'm here to try to understand what I am up against."

"Yes. My name is Janice and I'm not sure I belong here. My daughter, a sophomore in high school, is going to have a baby in a

month and we're not sure what is going to happen."

When families are thrust into kinship care three critical questions demand attention –

- How long will I be taking care of the children?
- When should I seek legal authority of the child?
- And what is the best legal authority for our situation?

First we'll look at these questions in the two main ways that children come to live with relatives, then we'll take a more in depth look at what the two main ways mean. All of this leads up to the types of authority relative care providers may want to consider. Finally, the last section of this chapter will offer some ways to make a decision on the caregiver authority choices.

Two Main Ways

The above questions are answered best when we understand the two main ways that children come to live with their relatives instead of their parents. Once again, naming in kinship care is still up for discussion among folks who work in social services. As you research Kinship Care you will find social pundits have named a variety of categories for types of care. The following two main ways with a slight addition to each are presented here so we can discuss the various programs and decisions that affect family decision makers:

- **Voluntary (basically informal)** – a request from parents or police in cases of accident.
  Voluntary formal refers to situations, without child welfare agency intervention, where relatives voluntarily seek to formalize the arrangement through the courts.

- **Placement (formal)** - a temporary or relative placement through a child welfare agency such as placement by Child Protective Services, (CPS). *Kinship Foster Care* (Relative <u>Foster Care</u>) could follow temporary agency kinship placements. The relative caregiver becomes a licensed Foster Care provider by the child welfare system.

Now let's look at those questions:

How long will I be taking care of the children?

This first difficult question involving the length of the children's stay frustrates many kin providers in both voluntary and agency placement situations.

In the case of some voluntary situations such as military deployment, a specific time has already been determined. Though the families may have to work through many of the same struggles as all kinship care situations - where the children sleep, allergies, being away from friends, anxiety of parental absence – the systems decisions such as legal authority of kin to care for the children can usually be worked out through careful planning with the parents for the term of the absence. Where actual legal authorization is an agreement between parents and caregiver, this may be considered a *voluntary formal* arrangement.

If the voluntary care of children is open-ended, however, ("for a little while"), the questions of how to maneuver through daily life can be haunting.

Placement always involves a child protective services agency who will also ultimately determine the length of time that children stay in placement. The agency will work with the parents and the caregivers to improve the situation that caused placement to happen. This could take just a few weeks. If improvement does not occur in the opinion of the agency, the length of time will be longer as other decisions are made (more permanent placement including foster care;

more on this later in the chapters).

When should I seek legal authority of the child?

The question in voluntary care can only be answered by the family. Care off and on for a few days because of a parent's job requirements should begin with the Medical Consent form (a sample follows in section II of this chapter). However, the family should also be aware of the requirements and needs for documentation of other systems that the children are involved in such as school or medical care.

When children are placed with a family by a child welfare agency, many of the questions about legal authority will be determined as the placement situation progresses.

What is the best documented authority for our situation?

Documented authority issues cover decisions on the child's behalf ranging from Medical Consent to Adoption. Please note that rules for legal options vary from State to State and from various jurisdictions within States. Some rules are established under Federal legislation. What we can offer here is an overview of what legal authority choices might be available for families trying to make long term decisions. Some of the names for legal authority in various states may also differ. Grandfamilies are urged to check out the options in their state and region before making decisions on their legal ties to the children. See the resource list in Section IV titled, of course, Resources.

Following is an in-depth look at the situations - *voluntary* and *placement*.

Voluntary Kinship Care Families

If we dare to call anything about kinship care traditional it would be the long history of relatives absorbing the care of children in the extended family. For as long as we have walked the earth together we have taken care of each other's children. Military or other job relocation or incarceration of parents often necessitates that relatives, particularly grandparents, care for the children during a specific period of time. "Yes, of course," is usually the answer to the question, "Will you take care of the kids?" Too often the agreement ends there without the "fuss" as one grandmother called it, of any written agreement.

However, today, in our culture, when children are left with grandparents or other relatives for an undetermined period of time without written authority, both children and caregivers become vulnerable to dynamics that threaten the security of the child.

The national numbers of voluntary kinship care without any documented authorization or child welfare involvement is not clear. Some sources have estimated that more than half of the millions of children cared for by a relative are in their relatives' homes without written authority to make decisions for the children. The consequences of no legal authority can be especially frustrating for relatives with good intentions.

Other Voluntary Kinship Care Situations and documentation considerations:
When the parent lives in the home of grandparents.

Grandparents raising teens and babies:

Some grandparents find themselves in the situation of raising their teenager *and* the teenager's baby. By the time mom and baby are home any discussions of outside adoptions or pregnancy termination are history. However, resolution of *who* is parenting the baby may not yet be settled. In the eyes of the law a teen parent living at the home of her parents is still the responsible parent of the newborn unless other arrangements are made such as grandparent as temporary or limited guardian or grandparent becoming the adoptive parent. Some families opt for a guardianship or power of attorney for the baby because the teen is not ready to parent.

Grandparents with teen parents most likely proceed through the experience cautiously and address needs as they arise. Babysitting by the grandparent may increase, therefore if no other authority documentation is implemented, *parents must remember to provide a Medical Consent form for emergency care (sample following).*

Trauma or illness of parent:

Other situations of the parent living in the home with the grandparent (or other relative's home) may find some form of legal guardianship in everybody's interest, such as a parent's debilitation through accident or disease and unable to care for themselves or their children. For example, if a parent is dying in a hospice situation, a Stand-by Guardianship, (kinship providing care without terminating parent's rights) and a plan for the future of the children's care should be considered.

Adele remembers the night she received the phone call from the State Police that her son-in-law had been killed and daughter severely injured in an auto accident. She needed to pick up the children from the babysitter. All of Adele's plans for shopping, visiting friends at her regular coffee gathering, and for volunteer work at the local elementary school were ended in one terrible moment. After discussion with the children's other grandparents, the three grieving young girls moved in with Adele. Several weeks later her daughter, the girls' mother, came from a respite care to Adele's home with severe head trauma and need of intensive care. Adele acquired a Stand-by Guardianship of the girls as well as her daughter and began the demanding effort of organizing insurances, medical payments, and the care of three youngsters.

In this case the children were not placed with Adele by a social services agency. Adele worked with the other grandparents to voluntarily assume the kinship care. Because the court is involved, but not a social services agency, this is another example of a voluntary formal situation.

Voluntary care is as different as each family situation. Sometimes kinship care becomes an extended family project with more than one family unit doing all the caring. Each family however, should look carefully at all of the legal options and services that can launch children into young adulthood with minimal grief.

Placement Situations

Josh and Jason, three-year-old twin boys, were found late one night holding hands, walking alone down a street several blocks from their parents' house. Police were called by a homeowner in the neighborhood. An investigation revealed not only the identity of the children, but also that the parents were manufacturing methamphetamine and were unaware of the children's disappearance. Child Protective Services removed the children from their parents' home charging child endangerment and neglect. The boys were placed with their grandmother who was granted temporary custody by order from the family court judge.

When children have been removed from parents by a child welfare agency for reasons of abuse or neglect charges, failure to protect or abandonment, usually a trusting relative is the first in sight for placement by the administering social services agency. This begins a unique partnership between the kinship care relative and the child welfare agency in the effort to secure the children in their parents' absence and, hopefully, to an eventually restored family situation.

Agencies providing placement services with kin consider these factors:

- the safety of the children with the kin
- the ability of the kin to take multiple children in a family,
- and the distance from the children's home.

Though not always a weighty factor, the trend, if possible,

of keeping children together and within a familiar distance means in their own "neighborhood", which may include the school they attend.

Placement is provided through the Children's Division of the State funded Department of Health and Human Services (often under a different name in different states, see the Resource). The actual placement service might come from another community program such as a Children's Services Agency, or a faith-based agency such as Catholic Social Services or Lutheran Children's Services. All outside agency placement services are under contract from the State Department of Health and Human Services and must, through State supervision, abide by the Federal legislative rules guiding child welfare.

Tribal placement policies are also administered under the various State's Children's Services. However, the Federal Indian Child Welfare Act (ICWA) of 1978 was enacted to address the "...alarmingly high percentage of Indian families . . . broken up by the removal, often unwarranted, of their children from . . . nontribal public and private agencies . . ." The ICWA requires States to establish rules for removal and placement of Indian children with full input by the tribe. The Act also requires States to provide for assistance to Indian tribes in the operation of child and family service programs. Through the Indian Child Welfare Act tribes are guaranteed the right to participate in and be key players in child welfare decisions that affect their tribe and its members. Children who are members of a recognized tribe or eligible for tribal membership are also assured placement under the care of their home tribe. (See resource list in Section IV). Kinship care families with questions regarding their possible native children or their State resources should begin with the placement agency or with the National Indian Child Welfare Association (www. nicwa.org).

Unlike voluntary care where much of the decision

making is initiated within the family, placement situations begin with child welfare involvement either through the Children's services division of the local Department of Health and Human Services (DHHS) or with an agency contracting through DHHS.

Formal placement or Relative Foster Care

In some cases where grandparents or other kin have a related child placed with them, the option of becoming a Relative Foster Care Parent may be offered to the relative caregiver. Becoming a Relative Foster Care Parent to related children may mean the same licensing process as non-related foster parents. Generally to be a licensed foster care provider requires a training program, scrutiny of the home, regular trainings, and travel restrictions. Also included is a permanency plan for the children in care. Some states have waived some of the foster care requirements for relative caregivers. Relative Foster Care is discussed in more detail in the chapter on the Trip to Social Services.

PART II:
Documented Authority for Kinship Care

All relatives or friends who agree to care for someone else's child will eventually face a need for some sort of documentation identifying written consent of authority from the parents or child welfare agency to make decisions for the child. In some situations that piece of official paper can mean the difference between getting help or not.

Obtaining documentation to protect children in a relative's home is critical. Though many families care for children without any written authority, the benefits of some documentation, though not legally binding, show a family's serious intent of care. In the case of a Medical Consent the document offers possible protection for medical care in emergency situations.

The benefits of *legally* binding protection (temporary placement custody, guardianship or adoption) include:

- Emergency medical care without frustrating delay or forcing parental entanglement with other public systems
- Smooth registration for school
- Social services benefits for the children
- Health care and health insurance coverage
- Protection from some custody disputes, which requires some form of court oversight to adjust, (parent cannot just come to reclaim the child)
- Child's own sense of security

Types of Documented Authority for care of kinship children:

Custody – Physical and Legal

First, a definition here about custody (which, once again, varies from state to state, check with a local legal resource on terminology before using these terms in a court): Generally, *Physical Custody* of a child simply means that the parent has verbally asked the relative to care for the child. No specified time or paperwork is involved. Physical Custody is *not* legally binding and will not be enough to secure some services for the children even getting into school. The parent can assume care of their child at any time. Again, there is no legal bond to keep the child with the relative. Unfortunately, the verbal "please take care of my child for awhile" without any written documentation is the way many kinship families are caring for their children.

Legal Custody refers to the adults who are legally responsible for children living with them. Parents are the Legal Custodians of their own children. Legal Custody

Authority Options for VOLUNTARY Relative Care of Children

Physical Custody	Care Permission Note	Power of Attorney	Guardianship	Adoption
No Documentation	Limited use for Medical decisions or School registration	Notarized, but not legally binding	Many types, all legal **in court** Limited, Temporary, Full, Stand-by	Caregiver has total parental rights
	Possible acceptance	Possible acceptance	Greater acceptance	Full acceptance
Parent has full rights	Parent has full rights	Parent has full rights	Guardian has most rights Any change must be in court	Parents rights terminated

Authority Options for Relative PLACEMENT Care of Children

Temporary Custody	Relative Foster Care	Permanent Custody	Adoption
Work with parents to reunite	If longer care necessary Work towards Permanency Plan	May include Guardianship in some states	Parental rights terminated

means taking responsibility for the child and making all important decisions for a child. When abuse or neglect occurs, Child Protective Services may remove the children temporarily and place the children in the Temporary Custody of a kin. The Temporary Custody is petitioned through the courts which may respond by limiting or restricting the parent's enjoyment of their presumed legal custody. With court ordered legal custody through an agency's temporary placement of children the assigned caregivers are responsible to fulfill the written court order that may include some restricted parental involvement with their child.

Medical Consent Note

Four-year-old Hunter was left one weekend with his maternal grandparents, Doris and Joe, while Mom and Dad attended an outdoor festival upstate. When Sunday night rolled around, grandparents heard nothing from their daughter. By Tuesday evening their daughter finally called saying she and Hunter's father would be gone a few more days.

Days turned into weeks with a scattered call here and there. Doris and Joe quietly cared for Hunter thinking their daughter would come for him any day now. When Hunter became sick Doris learned that the medical care required <u>parental signatures</u> to treat Hunter for Acute Asthma.

Suddenly for Joe and Doris caring for Hunter meant extensive medication and equipment, and worse, the discovery that they had no legal rights in his care. The hospital Emergency Room was required to call social services to authorize a responsible party for Hunter's medical care, in this case the grandparents were temporarily authorized.

Non-parent relatives or friends who bring a child to a hospital Emergency Room without written consent for treatment from the parents or other documented authorization are very likely to face delay in care for the child. If parents are not able to be contacted, additional delay and frustration occurs when the hospital and social services are required to seek legal intervention from Child Protective Services.

Some States require hospitals to inform local social services that the hospital emergency room staff will assume temporary parental authority in order to treat a child in serious medical danger. The child welfare agency may initiate child abandonment by the parents and arrange for temporary Guardianship or Custody (hopefully with the caring relative as in Hunter's case). In this type of situation, the parent(s) will then be required to prove to a family court judge that they have not abandoned their child.

This all may seem extreme, but the situation is serious enough that some states are enacting provisions for temporary medical authorization for child care providers. Under this serious concern, ***the primary step to securing a child even in the case of babysitting is to get a short Medical Consent Note dated and signed by the parent granting permission to the caregiver to make temporary medical decisions.*** For example:

---

date

If I am unable to be reached in case of a medical emergency, my mother (named), [or sister, Aunt, neighbor, etc] has my permission to provide emergency medical decisions for my child(ren), (named).

Signed by parent.

Such a note *may or may not be acceptable* by doctors or hospitals, but it is more likely to serve in an emergency than nothing. Many relatives have horror stories of medical professionals refusing to treat broken bones or internal ailments without the consent of the parent. Families in these cases face distress while children are taken under state custody leaving relative caregivers with no rights.

The trend for states to legislate a Medical Consent form through the child welfare agency is fast occurring. Check websites or social services offices of your state to see if a Medical Consent form is available for both parents and caregivers. Medical Consent form documents are like a Power of Attorney on a single issue. Read on.

Power of Attorney

Most states have a Uniform Probate Code, essentially laws that allow the power of attorney for one party to make decisions on behalf of another including a minor. Check with a local legal aid society, senior services center, or online legal forms for a Power of Attorney sample form. In a Power of Attorney document, parents can designate a relative to care for and make decisions on behalf of their children. Parents can even itemize what types of decisions the relative can make such as register the children for school, authorize medical or dental treatments, or protect funds for the child.

It isn't necessary, but having an attorney review the Power of Attorney can be valuable to correctness. Some attorney's will provide services pro bono (without charge) or legal aid services in the community may have an attorney on board to check your Power of Attorney document. The Power of Attorney document must be signed by both custodial parents and notarized by a Notary Public. Public service agencies, banks, and other resources often have someone who is certified as a Notary Public on staff. Notarizing is not required in some states, but it is recommended to show serious intent.

Though a parent can designate considerable authority to a relative in a Power of Attorney, the document is not always accepted by certain areas impacting a child's life such as most private health insurance providers and schools. A Power of

Attorney authority may also be limited in time according to each state's Uniform Probate Code definition. Michigan code, for instance, is limited to 6 months with an extension for military deployment. Ohio provides a one year Power of Attorney for kinship care. Other states simply require that the time be noted in the document. In some states the time limit may be renewed for as long as the parties consent.

Cooley Law School professors and the Statewide Kinship Care Focus Group of Michigan developed a a non-threatening consent-for-care form in a Kinship Care Resource Kit. The form is actually a Power of Attorney just for kinship care providers designed to soften the sometimes volatile issues between relatives over the care of the children. To copy the form go to www.michiganlegalaid.org. In the article search box type: Temporary Authorization for Kinship Care.

Kinship care providers must be very aware that the Power of Attorney can be withdrawn at any time by the parent(s). The Power of Attorney is *not* a legally binding document, but rather a written expression of intent. A Power of Attorney is not a court ordered guardianship, but may serve the children who are temporarily under the care of a relative.

Legal Documentations

Guardianships

Jane is a 30-year-old "career" woman whose life changed abruptly one summer when her sister, Sara, was ordered to enter a lengthy drug rehabilitation center. Sara informed the court that during her absence, sister Jane would care for Sara's 5-year-old daughter, Jessica. Sara never married, never revealed the identity of Jessica's father, and never solicited social services assistance.

Because Jane had enjoyed Jessica's company now and then on weekends, she thought this would be a simple adjustment. Jane had enough money, she thought, and they would work out longer term living arrangements such as sleeping, play area and other things belonging to Jessica. No one else needed to be involved.

Almost immediately Jane was faced with "involvement" of others. Jane's biggest concern was child care all day while she was at work. After considerable research in her urban area, she found a quality day care facility in the opposite direction from her work. She decided she could handle the travel time and the cost, one fourth of her income per week. She felt the expense was worth the quality of the care for Jessica.

Jane's resistance to involvement of outside institutions was challenged when she learned that the child care facility needed proof of Jane's legal authority to provide for her niece. This was more than a consent note – they needed guardianship or some legal bond that authorized Jane to make care decisions in the issues regarding little Jessica. The facility also needed medical records such as Birth Certificate and records of Jessica's childhood disease prevention schedule.

Jane back-tracked. Sara and Jane decided a Limited Guardianship in court would be the safest tie for Jessica and also show the court that Sara was making responsible decisions. They collected the few items of Jessica's baby records available. Jane had to take a couple of days off of work just to get through the maze of medical and legal information to place Jessica in quality, safe child care. Readers may want to check the chapter on Choosing Child Care.

Guardianship means that the caregiver is legally responsible for the care and protection of the child. With a legal guardianship, caregivers are able to access a number of services on behalf of the child. Guardianships have more clout with various services than Power of Attorney.

All guardianships require a trip to Family or Probate Court. Guardianships come in a variety of structures to fit various needs – Stand-by Guardianship for families facing an imminent death; Limited Guardianship with specific items and time frame noted; Temporary and Full Guardianships. The support of legal counsel to petition for guardianship can be invaluable though not always necessary. The transfer of parental authority from the parents to someone else, even a relative, can be an intimidating experience. Some courts may provide "do-it-yourself" packets for families with no legal counsel.

Many caregivers would rather not seek any guardianship because of the perceived trouble it may cause in the already troubled family. A Limited Guardianship, available in most states, is a temporary legal document that specifically states what portions of care the parent and caregiver can agree on. Limited Guardianship can be time-sensitive, that is, a deadline of the guardianship is usually written into the document. The Limited Guardianship is essentially a written agreement of specific items of care for a limited time, much like a Power of Attorney. The difference between Power of Attorney and Limited Guardianship is the court approval. Parents and guardians must go back to court for any changes including returning the children to parental authority. Under Power of Attorney parents can rescind the document at any time.

Limited Guardianships are especially useful for military families when a parent must be away for a specific time period and prefers to smooth the caregiver's path through service systems on behalf of the child.

Children in kinship care, either through voluntary or placement means, have greater advantages in longer term situations when a legal Temporary Custody or Full Guardianship is in place. Parents seeking the return of custody after rehabilitation or some return to normalcy for the parent-child family will have to provide evidence as to why they are now more able to care for their own child. Often the teen parent who gave guardianship to her parents for a baby finds maturity and security in her young adulthood and so must show evidence in court of her ability to raise her child in order to terminate the guardianship her parents held for her child.

All Guardianships, temporary or permanent, must be

filed in Probate Court with evidence of the care provided by the relative. In cases involving Child Protective Services (placement), where the social services workers of the child welfare agency expect longer term care for the children, a guardianship may be the course of action.

Adopting Kin

Once some type of Guardianship or Permanent Custody has been in place for an established period of time and it is clear that the children will not be returning to the parents, grandparents and other kin providers along with the children in their care may consider the advantages of adoption. Adoption is the most secure form of legal attachment for kinship families, it is the ultimate choice for children whose lives have been severely separated from the parents through death or long term separation. Adoption means that the caregiver becomes the parent in the eyes of the law and with all the advantages of parenting in the eyes of the community (and insurance providers).

Adoption is designed to be permanent. Children need permanency, a sense of security in their home. In some situations, Guardianship provides all the security needed in the perception of the children. Adoption is another choice. Many states provide a little or a lot of assistance with adoption of kin depending on the circumstances and the states statutes. Much more about the financial and social services help regarding adoption is discussed in the chapter titled the Trip to Social Services.

PART III:
Making the Legal Authority Decision

First a thought about resistance:

There are many reasons why caregivers just do the

job hoping they won't need public involvement in their situation. Resistance to entering anything "legal" or "social services" is strong especially when children are left in care "just for a little while," or when families think they have enough money to manage the situation, or they just don't want anyone knowing their business. Cultural values often inhibit families from securing some form of legal bond giving the caregiver authority to support the children. Some families are simply unaware that they may need any proof of care until faced with circumstances that seriously complicate the situation.

Often a grandparent fears that asking for a Power of Attorney or Limited Guardianship will strain an already damaged relationship with their children. Sometimes adult children can be intimidating or divisive increasing the guilt some grandparents are already experiencing. No matter what feelings prevail, situations regarding the children's safety must be confronted and a plan made to secure the children temporarily or long term.

The case is strong for securing children with a grandparent or other relatives through some form of *written* documentation.

Now you know there are many options to securing some form of documented and legal authority to make decisions for the child. But which one is best for your family?

In the case of Voluntary kinship care, some families start with the simple Medical Consent Form, while others prefer something a little more substantial like the Power of Attorney.

In the case of Placement, kinship care providers are in a partnership with the child welfare system. Generally the goal of placement is to secure the children safely while trying to change the problems that led to placement of the children away from the parents. The ultimate goal of placement is to reunite children with their parents safely. Legal authorization for relative caregivers begins with

Temporary custody signed by a Family Court judge while the child welfare agency works with the parents.

However, sadly, if after some time of working with the family, child welfare recognizes that parents may not be the safest place for their children and a more permanent placement is sought, usually with the relative caregiver. It is at this point that kinship care providers will need to consider the best legal option for their family security – usually permanent guardianship or adoption.

No matter how children come to live with their relatives, at some point the kinship care providers will eventually seek documented, probably legal, authority in order to make decisions on behalf of the child.

Guidebooks, counselors, good friends can help a relative make the decision of when and how to strengthen a legal attachment to the child.

Communities have many resources to help you in the decision making process. When the family is in dissention over child custody issues, seeking outside help may be the best route to securing the children. Dispute Resolution organizations often sponsored by courts or non-profits have trained professionals available to assist families struggling to get through the barriers of differences. When seeking out such helping resources, check for words like *Conflict Resolution* or *Dispute Resolution* or check with agencies that provide multiple services to families.

Some university Social Work Education departments are beginning to incorporate community training by offering decision making workshops presented by graduate students in the field. Michigan State University has a very unique child and family clinic operated by graduate students in the School of Social Work and the MSU School of Law. The program, *Chance at Childhood*, recognizes that both social workers and family law attorneys often collaborate on behalf of clients in a variety of family law situations. Chance at Childhood provides a hands-on opportunity for students to learn the subtle links between law and the social services structure by working with families across Michigan on actual custody, child maltreatment, and kinship law cases, www.chanceatchildhood.msu.edu. This unique community clinic is a model for other university programming in Social Work and Law.

Another source for decision making regarding the best authority documentation for kinship families is the local Kinship Care Center. Staff of a comprehensive service program can help families to look objectively at their situation through some practical decision making techniques. In the text box is a story of one such technique, a third party response from a local Kinship Care coordinator.

Whether your initial decision is a Medical Consent form, Power of Attorney, legally binding guardianship, or ultimately adoption, the process of making a legal authorization decision can be very challenging. Remember, most choices can be changed if they do not work out. The important rule here is to do what you can to secure the children during their stay under relative care by thoughtfully acting on some form of documentation that identifies your authorization to care for the child.

A Third Party Technique

Anna and John used a Third Party technique to begin the process of decision-making for their grandson. Like Margaret, Anna and John experienced off and on care for their young grandson during their daughter's sporadic visits. Anna went to her Kinship Care Center coordinator for suggestions. The coordinator offered to facilitate a non-legal Agreement as a tool to open discussion with the mother and father and grandparents of little Timmy. The 17-year-old mother was still exploring her own adolescence and the father was a boy living in a nearby town who just wanted to see his son now and then even though he and the mother were no longer a couple.

Anna arranged a meeting at her house with the mother, father and the Kinship care Coordinator to discuss some specific issues regarding Timmy's care. The young parents were required for the first time to think about the costs to Anna and John, medical care for Timmy and possible insurance coverage, and importantly specific parenting time with Timmy. The Kinship Care Coordinator prepared a non-binding document based on the family discussion where everyone agreed to how much money they would provide Anna and John, the process for making medical decisions for Timmy, and assured times for visits with their son including paternal grandparents. All signed the document noting that this was a <u>non-binding</u> Agreement intended to simply make everyone aware of the issues involved in the early years of raising this child.

Ultimately, Anna and John acquired a guardianship for Timmy as both his parents moved on to separate lives. The parents responsibility to their son, however, was defined more easily in the guardianship as a result of the Agreement two years before.

The Trip to
Social Services

As the social worker described the many services to John regarding his kinship care to three grandchildren, John's mind went into a fog, that's how John later described his first trip to the Social Services department after the children had been left in his care. "I had my wallet with all my identification. What else would I need? I figured they would tell me how long I would have the kids and when the court dates were. I was actually overwhelmed with the thought of caring for three children by myself. I only agreed because there was no one else. The kids and I had a good relationship and I wasn't about to let them go to strangers." John learned that there was a little money available to help with the extra expenses, that down the road he might need to think about guardianship depending on how things worked out. He was given a packet of community services as well as programs from the Department of Health and Human Services and each child received a Medicaid card. Then they began to ask questions – about the children's health, whether he would need public assistance which meant bringing more papers. "I wish I had known more about the system when I went in – it would have saved a lot of time and agony."

State and community supported social services for individuals and families are conducted and funded through the Federal and State Department of Health and Human Services (DHHS), sometimes known by different names in different states. Child Protective Services (CPS), a department within DHHS responds to emergency child welfare situations and other juvenile concerns. "Child welfare agency" and "social services" are part of the same social services structure discussed here. See the Resources for various states' names of the DHHS office.

As we have discussed, children come to relative care in one of two ways, briefly:

- Voluntary – the parent or other non-agency source asks the relative to care for the child
- Placement – the child welfare agency has removed the child from the home for child abuse or neglect and *placed* the child with a willing relative.

The relative's involvement with social services will differ depending on which of these two ways children have come to the relative's home.

Voluntary – Kinship Care Families & Social Services

Families in voluntary kinship care may never need social services. A parent asks grandma to take care of the baby for a while. Parent and grandma get a Medical Consent signed or a Power of Attorney or other written legal authorization (see Becoming a Kinship Care Provider). Parent gives grandma money to help cover expenses and goes away for awhile. Parent comes back and resumes parenting. Grandma does not need community financial support or medical help for grandchild. No social services involvement. Imagine that.

About .001% of Kinship Care families experience such a smooth caring experience.

Unfortunately most families are caught up in bigger dynamics too often involving alcohol or drugs, or systems that are not very supportive of Kinship Care such as insurance companies. Relatives who voluntarily accept children are faced with many situations that may require outside help:

- babies with fetal alcohol syndrome
- toddlers who have experienced domestic violence in their home
- parents who come and go from the children's lives with little regard for the emotional roller coaster on the children
- financial burdens for food, transportation, medical needs for children or relatives.

Voluntary kinship care providers will find that the huge social services system in their community (though frustrating at times) can offer a wide range of services or connections to other community services.

Some of the services that are likely provided by your local Social Services Department:

- **Child-only grants,** is a designated amount of monthly cash to support children in kinship care without including the relative's income These funds are known by many different names including: ineligible grantees, personal needs, or child-only assistance. The amount provided varies. In some states it is not the same for each child in the home, but may decrease by the number of children in care or may be a single amount regardless of the number of children in the home.
- **Child care supplemental funds,** particularly for

relatives with out-of-the-home jobs. In many cases this supplement can be calculated without including the relative's income.

- **Medicaid for the children,** or an eligibility for (SCHIP – State Children's Health Insurance Program) a State supported insurance for children who cannot for some reason receive Medicaid. Unfortunately, too many health insurance providers will not include kinship children regardless of the legal authorization short of adoption. The advantages of Medicaid or a State insurance for the child means immunizations, medications, sometimes dental, and referral for special medical needs. Having the Medicaid or State Health Insurance card for the children offers a passport to services for many special medical needs. Note that State Children's Health Insurance Program has different names for different states and not all states participate in the program.

- **Legal authority assistance,** a social services connections for voluntary situations or placement, may include assistance or referral in obtaining guardianship or other legal authority to secure the child (see the section on Legal Options).

- **General help with stuff,** some social services departments become the vehicle for community service projects such as Holiday Angel gifts, back to school supplies, subsidies or other programs for clothes, baby equipment, etc. available to families once children are in the social services system.

- **Public assistance,** such as Food Stamps or other food voucher subsidy programs funded through Temporary Assistance to Needy Families (TANF). This is part of the new welfare reform act that reviews the grandparent or relative's income. General public assistance comes with a wide variety of rules depending on the relative's resident state response to the Federal welfare reform act legislation (Personal Responsibility and Work Opportunity Reconciliation Act of 1997). The Act requires "grantees" to work off the grant amount. Social caseworkers and the community help to find the jobs for this stipulation. If the relative is considered a "senior" (60, 62, 65 depending on the agency) the eligibility for financial support which includes Food Stamps (Vouchers or Card) may waive the welfare-to-work rule. There are other requirements in some states including the limited lifetime acceptance of assistance. Some states even require a drug test to receive assistance. Many of these requirements may be waived for kinship care providers. More on public assistance later in this chapter.

- **Foster care licensing.** Usually in the cases involving Placement, Relative Foster Care may be offered. This is explained further in the Placement section of this chapter. The advantage is that Relative Foster Care for children who have little chance of returning to their parent's home provides the kinship family with a firm, amount of money for each child placed in the relative's home. Under new rules, Relative Foster Care is also likely to enforce strict home review, parental trainings, and other involvement.

- **Guardianship subsidy payments.** Many states are now developing financial support for kinship care families through the Adoption and Safe Families Act. The subsidy amount is usually not as high as foster care, but substantially more support than the child-only assistance. These funds are legislated by states, often under the name of Guardianship Subsidy Act. The amount of subsidy and the rules of eligibility vary considerably from State to State. Kinship providers are usually clearly defined in the Act. The subsidy can be a significant assistance for families who have legal custody of kinship children. States that have or have had Kinship Guardianship Subsidies are noted in the Social Service Listings in the Resources Section of the book.

- **Adoption assistance.** Through the Department of Health and Human Services a variety of adoption assistance may be available to kinship care families from financial support to post adoption counseling. The local social services may have a specific worker or department that can assist relatives with questions regarding adoption of their kin child. For more federal information, check with Child Welfare Information Gateway, the information center of the federal Children's Bureau. Once on this website a number of options regarding adoption are available, http://www.childwelfare.gov. More discussion about kinship care adoption is noted later in this chapter.

- **Tribal eligibility assistance.** If you live in a state that has an active Indian population, questions about children and tribal issues including eligibility may be available through a specific worker that specializes in Indian Social Services. If you do not have a local information source check with the National Indian Child Welfare Association, www.nicwa.org.

Voluntary kinship care providers that are facing difficulty with money, medical or legal concerns should contact their social services department and inquire about assistance. Advocating on behalf of children and the experience of kinship care can be very beneficial from social services assistance programs.

Placement – Kinship Care Families & Social Services

Families who receive a child through placement from a child welfare agency will be involved with social services in a somewhat different experience than voluntary kinship care families. Though placement families will be offered many of the above services, they will also become partners with social services to assist the parents in changing the circumstances that led to the removal of the children. That partnership may include cooperating with court approved visits for parents and children, court or counseling appointments and possibly some specialty care (for example, counseling for sexually abused children).

As the placement process moves forward caregivers may be preparing children to return to their parents or to take a more permanent status as kinship care providers. When child welfare determines that children will not be safe with their parents, other arrangements will be considered.

Relative Foster Care

One option to kinship caregivers is Relative Foster Care. Since the 1980's the increase in Relative Foster Care has been significant. More than one-fourth of the children currently in the country's Foster Care system are living with a relative.

As Relative Foster Care *licensed* providers, kinship care families can receive considerably more support for the children than the gray area of "kinship placement" or temporary placement. Unfortunately, recent studies show that the Foster Care payments are far below the serious cost of raising children. That topic is under consideration in the political arena. The licensing for Relative Foster Care varies from state to state where kinship placements are concerned. Some states require the full shot of approved homes – space and number of bedrooms for numbers of children, family income, training of the foster parents, and on-going training. Licensed Relative Foster Care homes are often on the state "roster" and may be asked to take other non-related children. Some states on the other hand, do not apply non-relative foster care licensing to Relative Foster Care families.

One of the key issues of Foster Care is the development of

a *Permanency Plan* for the children, often with the outcome of permanency placement determined within 12 months. This too, varies by state, and by case within states. However, the possible impact of a Permanency Plan for children in Relative Foster Care may mean that all parties involved with securing the children – the child welfare agency, the relative caregivers, and even the children should be considering future options as everyone progresses through the placement.

Relative Foster Care, for instance, could progress to Guardianship or Adoption, though even in this situation some state rules prohibit Foster Care providers from adopting the children in care. Sounds crazy, but all of these "possible", "may", "varies by state" words means kinship care providers, Voluntary or Placement, must also be advocates for their family when it comes to public systems and *be prepared to ask questions,* ("Does our State have a Guardianship subsidy? Who is eligible? What are the rules for Relative Foster Care in our state?" etc).

Tribal Placement

If the child is a member of a federally recognized Indian tribe or eligible for membership in a tribe, an additional set of placement concerns enters the picture. Relatives who accept initial placement, whether the relative is tribal or non-tribal, should be prepared to understand the public systems involved in the longer term placement of the child and work together with the agencies involved for the best interests *of the child.*

What a relative might expect on the first trip to Social Services.

Schedule the meeting with the social services worker, (or the first meeting may be scheduled for the caregiver in situations of emergency placement).

Eat a good breakfast, arrange child care if necessary,

bring something to do in case you have to wait. In fact, plan on waiting.

Bring papers (see the list below), a notebook and pen (see Getting Organized).

Be prepared to ask questions. Remember there is a vast difference between the policies of states and even within the county/parish jurisdictions of individual states, which is why asking questions is so important. Even some child welfare workers may not know some of the services available or how to access the services.

Consider bringing some of the following papers to the meeting. Relatives don't have to haul all the papers out during the meeting, just have them available in case they are needed. The list may seem daunting especially if relatives received the children under urgent conditions. It is silly to say to a parent going to jail that you need some of the papers here. This is a working list of possibles.

- If possible, bring <u>social security numbers</u> for all directly involved – children, relative provider, and parents
- <u>Birth certificates</u> for children,
- <u>Legal authorization papers -</u> power of attorney or guardianships, even consent for care note, if available.
- <u>Proof of income</u> in the *relative's home* – such as recent pay receipts or check stubs, pension statements, social security statement or electronic deposit statement from the relative's bank, the previous year's IRS statement. This is just in case the relative applies for assistance.
- <u>Household expenses</u> particularly utilities and rent.
- Any <u>medical papers regarding the child</u> such as immunizations, family doctor or health department case numbers for the child, or any medical diagnosis for chronic disabilities.

Though this all sounds invasive into the relative's privacy, it is likely that the only relevant numbers will be the social security numbers. Being prepared can mean less trips and less frustration.

The choices made by grandparents and other relatives on the trip to social services for kinship care will depend on whether children are in the home through *placement* or *voluntary*.

If a placement has been made, especially on an emergency basis, the relative's first in-office experience with social services may already be planned by the case worker. The relative may be offered a foster care program, though probably not on the early visits. Non-foster care kinship placement is likely to include child-only assistance, Medicaid for the child, and a possible discussion of other elements of the child's life such as school or special needs. In cases of physical or sexual abuse counseling services may be offered or even required as well.

The relative care giver may want to ask several questions at this point depending on the situation. Don't forget to take notes.

General Questions
- What is the difference between the general kinship placement and foster care licensing?
- What is the time frame for the Placement (or Foster Care)? In other words, what happens next? Is this a permanent situation? Who does the supervising for parental visits? What are the housing and training rules for Foster Care? Could the parents lose their rights to the child?
- What is the child-only grant? Kinship care families that are caring for children in temporary placement are eligible for some aid in most states particularly through the child-only assistance, that is, a small sum of money for the children each month and a Medicaid card for each child. Ask about this program,

some workers may not be aware of the child-only assistance.

- What are the benefits of the Medicaid card? What are the restrictions? Ask about medical availability with the Medicaid card. Many doctors or clinics do not accept Medicaid requiring relatives to plan appointments more carefully to Medicaid clinics considering especially travel time and transportation.

Public Assistance Questions

If the relative is surviving on low income and seeks to apply for public assistance for food vouchers and other financial aid, questions on the assistance program (Personal Responsibility and Work Opportunity Reconciliation Act) should be covered carefully before any papers are signed:

- Will the grandparent or relative have to work outside the home to pay for the grant? Does the agency provide assistance getting the job? Is child care available or assistance to pay for child care?
- How much will the assistance be compared to the child-only income? (In other words, is it worth it?)
- Is there a time limit for assistance? This is a critical question. A grandmother at 62 years of age, with two young children, who can only apply for 60 months cap on assistance may face extreme difficulty at 67 when the children are still in elementary school. Many States are trying to adjust the time-limit rule to accommodate kinship care providers. Ask.
- Will social services pursue child support from the parents of the kinship children if I apply for public assistance beyond the child-only grant? This is an important question for many families. In many states the public assistance for voluntary kin caregivers requires social services to collect child support from the parents. This ruling often inhibits relatives who

could use the financial help from applying for public assistance because they do not want more dissention in the family.

Guardianship and Guardianship Assistance Questions

- How to get the guardianship established? What type of guardianship?
- Does the state provide a Kinship Care or Guardianship Subsidy? What are the rules to obtain the subsidy? Some subsidies have requirements as to the length of time the child has been with the relative, age of the child, children coming from foster care only, or families possessing guardianship papers only. Because Kinship Care subsidies are a new and growing trend to support the valuable care giving of relatives, the rules vary widely by state. In some states only grandparents can apply (what??). For some, the subsidy is only available for children under 12. It is important to ask if a relative subsidy is available and what are the eligibility rules.

Subsidy parameters are tied closely to the funds available in state social services budgets. The whole concept has only been in existence a few years and in only a few states, though the support is growing. Relatives should ask about the kinship subsidy and know the specific restrictions in their state. Keep in mind this is not a hand-out – relatives across the country are saving tens of thousands of dollars in communities by securing children that will not have to go to costly Foster Care or Residential Care. See the Resources Section for a list of states with some sort of Guardianship Assistance Subsidy.

Closing the Interview

Once a plan is in place for kinship care of the children, the relative will also need to know that they can contact the worker to answer questions or change directions in the care situation. Contact numbers, *with alternate numbers* and names, should be obtained and put in two or three places in the home (see Getting Organized). Subsequent trips to social services are inevitable especially as the parent situation progresses. Take time to file notes and papers resulting from social services visits.

What all this means to the grandparent or aunt or older brother or cousin or godparent who is involved with the social services agency is to *ask questions*. ASK QUESTIONS and listen to answers. Repeat the answers back to the social worker to be sure you both understand what the answers mean. Confirm your meeting of questions and answers in writing. In other words send a letter within a day or two after the meeting to the social service worker. For example:

"Dear ---, Thank you for your efforts on behalf of my grandchildren and myself on (date of the meeting). I am sending this note to be sure I understand what the results of the meeting are – (then list the items) you will do this and that.

I will get this and that for you by such and such a date.

Again thank you for your help during this family adjustment."

Sign and date the letter and MAKE A COPY before you send it.

The social services choices available to kinship providers require careful consideration. The benefits can be very helpful. Remember we all have the same goal: to secure each child in a safety net that is predictably permanent and that enhances the child's well-being. Agencies and kinship providers can work together on the foundation of that clear goal.

Other
Community Services

Liz, a young grandmother guardian to infant Jason, followed her social services worker suggestion to see what the Early On program had to offer her tiny grandson. She bundled him up in the best baby clothes she could and took him to the Intermediate School Building where the Early On program was one of many services offered to schools and families. Jason was not an active baby. His birth mother was alcohol and drug addicted leaving Jason with some possible scary outcomes in his mental and physical development. What Liz found in the Early On program was much more than she ever believed existed. Professionals worked with her on nutrition and physical issues for Jason. They arranged for specific medical treatment in the initial first year of his life – the brain development year. And they taught Liz the gentle art of infant massage. "I couldn't believe it," Liz said later, "little Jason just lay listless until we learned together what a wonderful awakening infant massage could be. It wasn't just for him. I think we bonded more during those sessions and later on than we ever could have if I hadn't gone to the Early On program." Later Liz attended classes on Fetal Alcohol Syndrome and ultimately became a leader in her local Early On program.

We've already discussed the essentials of your local **Social Services Department (Department of Health and Human Services - DHHS)** and the many areas of help from this valuable public service. There are many other resources in most communities around the country offering programs from infant care to mental health.

Following is a brief list of other essential public services that may be of value to the relative who is seeking specific assistance. Again, these services are often cooperatively funded by Federal, State, and local resources and may have different names or operate as programs under different organizations. Head Start, for instance, that exceptional pre-school program, is managed by a variety of different organizations such as schools, community services (Community Action Agency), even churches.

Many community organizations are working more effectively together and have developed information resources directories. The community information service number, 2-1-1 (like 9-1-1 for emergency services) is becoming a key resource for communities across the country. This number operates with a live person that helps callers to find the local source they need. Check the website www.211.org to see if a 211 service exists in your area. The comprehensive number is a project of United Ways Alliance for Information and Referral Systems. You can also check with your local United Way for more information on locations of the service.

Several public organizations offer a great number of services within their expertise such as the Community Health Department which serves the health needs of infants to the very elderly. In addition, several non-profit organizations on very specialized issues such as Diabetes, can be a good information resource in the community. Some of these specialized areas are listed through a national toll-free number. Caregivers, in their new role as advocate, should search locally first for assistance, then try general information resources such as the U.S. Government publications and forms, www.usa.gov (1.800.333.4636 or 800 FED INFO) for information on business, non-profits, citizen concerns. Also check out www.pueblo.gsa.gov for the consumer bulletins on a number of areas that we all use – cars, money, education – explore the site online for a more complete understanding of what is available, mostly free from Federal Citizen Information Center (1.888.878.3256 or 1.888.8PUEBLO).

A few communities have collaborated to produce an easy inexpensive, highly effective route for folks to search out family resource: The Children's Yellow Pages – a simple brochure printed on yellow paper listing telephone numbers of specialized resources by category. Printing is cheap for these handy community service directories. In our new world of computer use, maintenance of the list is easy, and distribution of the directory to public places is done by volunteers.

Following is an overview of some mainstream organizations and how they may be of service to grandparents and other non-parent relatives raising children.

Child Abuse Reporting – check with the local department of social services. Teachers, doctors, dentists, and other professionals who work with children may be required by the state to report suspected child abuse or neglect.

Child Abuse Prevention – communities fortunate enough to have a child abuse prevention program have an excellent resource to several organizations and ways they can help all families. A Child Abuse and Neglect Prevention program exists to educate communities and work with parenting programs to prevent abuse and neglect.

Community Mental Health – Federally and state funded Community Mental Health centers provide therapy services to the community. Some education services are available as well. A solid community mental health service offers a wide range of therapeutic help from substance abuse to adolescent issues and residential referral, (see the chapter on Counseling).

Community Action Agency – funded through Federal Community Block Grants and state and local sources, community action agencies are designed to address the local needs of the communities experiencing poverty. Services can include neighborhood development, transportation, children's issues (such as Head Start), home heating, literacy, financial education, and financial assistance. Self-sufficiency is a key to the work of the Community Action Agency. Hundreds of communities across the country have been lifted out of the energy drain of poverty through the efforts of these effective organizations.

Domestic Violence Prevention and Assault Shelters – Shelters for victims of domestic assault, both physical and mental, survive on community support as non-profit organizations. The shelters offer not only protection but also counseling (including for non-residents of the shelter), transitional programs (helping victims build a new life), children's programs, and community education.

Early On - also by many other names, this early childhood program provides services to families with infants to three years old (where little ones may move into Head Start). Early On could be offered through a public education source such as an Intermediate School District, or as a part of another community organization that supports family and children programs. Services of Early On include educational programs and development for young children and their caregivers. Educational programs may use recognized early childhood research and development such as *Zero to Three* (or *Zero to Three* might be a separate program in the community). These programs are the best source for understanding the crucial issues of early brain development and the effect on the potential of the growing child (who ultimately becomes a citizen of the community). Issues that affect the brain include fetal alcohol syndrome, drug addicted babies, infant and toddler chronic birth issues, visual and hearing impaired, just to mention a few.

Head Start – This is the champion of early childhood development programs providing support for underserved families (including relatives). Head Start is generally a comprehensive family program for 4-year olds with some boosts for 3-year-olds and 5- year-olds in targeted populations where no other pre-head start program exists. Head Start consists of educational time for the children, home visits and strong support for families, and parent support. Alums of Head Start programs, adults now, are vital members of communities across the country. This is a program America can be proud to claim.

Health Department – One of the most essential programs in any community, often housed in the same area as Social Services and/or Community Mental Health, the Public Health Departments have a wide range of programs that promote the health of all citizens. Children's programs may include immunization clinics, visiting nurses for new moms, diagnostic recognition of special needs including referral and possible financial support. The Health Department also works to prevent communicable diseases – flu, norovirus, and sexually transmitted diseases. Elder health is also a component of many Health Department services.

Intermediate School District (ISD) – Not in every state and often under the budget gun in the states where the districts exist. The ISD's are a strong central source particularly in rural counties where consolidation of materials and services can be efficient and networked to smaller schools in the district, including testing for vision and hearing, ADD, and other learning interferences. Early On is often a program of the ISD as well as programs for children with severe mental or emotional disabilities who are not ready for general classroom work.

Kinship Care Resource Center – This is the most important referral source for Relatives As Parents, Grandparents Raising Grandchildren, etc. The Kinship Resource Center may be an independent non-profit or operate under the care of another agency such as the Department on Aging or Senior Center. An entire section of this book is devoted to strengthening or developing a Comprehensive Kinship Care Resource Center.

Schools – The local school can be a treasure of resources to help the kinship care provider. Schools offer special services that will enhance the educational potential of students such as visual and hearing testing. There are after-school programs, before school programs often with food. Free and reduced lunches. Many extra-curricular activities from sports to performing arts to science clubs. Families who are able to take advantage of these special activities could open up a wide range of experiences for youngsters that take the focus away from family difficulties. See the chapter on Working with Schools.

Senior Center – Many senior programs have recognized the impact of grandparents and other older relatives who are raising their related children. Through federal and state organizations serving aging citizens, appropriations have been incentives to local groups to establish comprehensive kinship care resource services. See the chapter on Comprehensive Kinship Care Resource Centers. In addition, senior services centers often offer an extensive array of services to the older population including fitness centers, nutrition programs, tax assistance, specific health support, meals, and a social environment with peers.

University Extension Offices – A few years ago, state universities through their Schools of Social Work began to address the needs of kinship care services. Programs were designed to educate folks in local communities through the extension offices of the University. In many states the education led to establishing support programs and outreach services to kinship care providers. Some of the leading University Extension programs are listed in this book. Check with your own prominent universities for kinship care programs. Communities where university or colleges exist can also offer services specifically for youth that greatly help kinship families.

Youth Programs – YMCA, Big Brothers/Big Sisters, Boys And Girls Clubs, 4-H, – Youth programs are another valuable support for kinship families. In some areas the YMCA will be the umbrella non-profit for extended kinship care services. Other youth organizations offer mentoring, tutors, clubs and fun "learning" experiences such as job preparation or study helps.

Churches, Mosques, Temples, - where ever a strong faith based facility exists, a number of services can be addressed that directly affect kinship care providers from providing a place where caregivers can meet to offering children's programs.

There are many resources in communities not named here such as specific ethnic or cultural centers, neighborhood programs, projects of service clubs like Kiwanis, Rotary, Optimists, Lions, etc. There is no reason for kinship families to suffer difficulties alone. Now is the time to reach out and accept the extended community hand.

When to Seek
Counseling

When Margaret heard the knock at the door, she instinctively knew this was it, her dreaded concern for grandsons Tyrone and James. The police officer and social worker that escorted the boys to Margaret's home explained that the parents had been arrested for assault and abuse of the children. The boys ran to their grandmother clinging close to her throughout the night. Margaret learned later that a number of people were at the house drinking and using drugs before the fights that left the children terrorized. As the weeks went by, Margaret was concerned that her boys, especially the youngest one, James, could not be left alone. He would shake all over, cry and beg to sleep with his brother in the same little twin bed, or better, sleep with Margaret. He would not even go to the bathroom alone. James and Tyrone were eligible for counseling funds through the Department of Social Services placement program, transportation support to therapy was also provided to Margaret and the boys. As the counseling sessions progressed a terrible revelation occurred – someone at the party played Russian Roulette with a gun to James' head causing a nearly deadly foray and ultimate police intervention.

Though this terrible situation identifies the importance of good therapy, just leaving a parent's home can be trauma enough for children. Some situations may need the aid of intensive child therapy to get through the effects of abuse and neglect. When the psychological damages of severe abuse or neglect are not checked by corrective therapy, the whole society might pay for the outcomes. We all know that abuse can go through the generations like a curse. We also know that quality therapy can greatly reduce the terror and offer an end to abuse and a beginning to a quality life.

In this section we will briefly explain what some of the causes and results of various kinds of trauma and conditions have on children including abuse, neglect and some physical effects of drugs, alcohol and infections from birth. This is a very limited overview of some of the conditions that kinship care families experience. Seeking help and becoming an advocate for children is critical. Caregivers also need help. The stress of caring for children in trauma can be exhausting. There are many resources for specific areas, but grandparents and all caregivers must take the initiative to get the help needed. The terms *counseling* and *therapy* are the same throughout this chapter.

A Profile of the Effects of Abuse

The human brain of every baby is like a massive computer taking in data, analyzing, categorizing. Unlike a computer, the developing human experiments with the information, repeating sounds, testing new senses, practicing humor. This process takes place through the miracle of biochemistry – proteins flushing throughout the system building little electronic brain bridges to intelligence. This marvelous creature requires more than information. Positive interaction with a baby's "people" assures healthy development. Nutrition and rest are equally as important. All the greatness of healthy development can only take place without fear in the secure safety of a loving home.

When babies are subjected to *constant* stress through denial of basic needs, or worse, through abusive actions of the caregivers they trust – yelling, hitting, burning – the developing brain becomes awash in the stress chemical, *cortisal*, which can ultimately stop the development and create some frightening child responses: failure to thrive, inconsolable, or a lack of empathy.

- **Failure to thrive** is a diagnosis for babies that are not growing and developing in a normal progression. It is not always the consequence of neglect. Some failure to thrive occurs as a result of other physical problems.
- **Inconsolable** is a chronic mournful crying not like "colic" or crying for attention to a need, but rather a melancholy sadness, unable to respond to adult care and loving attention.
- **Lack of empathy** is a very rare but serious psychological response to abuse or neglect that eventually results in a human able to commit crimes against others without remorse or empathy.

Though the earliest years of development are the most active for organizing in the human personality, traumatic events that occur later in a child's life can have the same effect of stunted growth, scattered memory, repressed anger, aggressiveness, or withdrawn. These barriers to the development of the child are compounded by a personal sense of guilt, unworthiness, or as our society catch-phrases – a low self-esteem.

Children suffering from the untreated effects of child maltreatment carry the burden into their school years, limiting their educational growth, falling behind in basic concepts of reading, calculating, and the fun of educational curiosity. This adds to their low-self-esteem which could eventually lead to dropping out of school and taking the bumpy road through life.

Child abuse and neglect are devastating barriers to a growing child, (an average of three children die in our country *every day* through abuse or neglect). Sometimes other barriers also affect these beautiful little creatures. Relative caregivers should be aware of the impact a number of conditions have on children. Following is a very sketchy reference to some of these syndromes, disorders, and physical conditions.

Fetal Alcohol Syndrome (FAS) (a part of medically identified Fetal Alcohol Spectrum of Disorders)

Too many babies are born with the affects of their birth mother's alcohol or drug addiction which ultimately impacts the brain developing in the womb and the baby trying to overcome this crippling barrier to their growth process. This is a condition that is 100% preventable.

Studies show that the effects of alcohol on the baby are different at different times in the development when the alcohol goes through the placenta limiting oxygen to the baby and nourishment for the critical cell growth in the brain and body. This is why professionals say taking alcohol any time during pregnancy is dangerous.

Some of the symptoms of Fetal Alcohol Syndrome (FAS) can include a smaller body, slower development, bone and joint deformities, missing fingers/toes, or fused or webbed toes. FAS may sometimes be detected through facial abnormalities such as small eye openings or difficulty with eyelids and eyes. Noses and jaws, poorly formed ears can all be affected. Some FAS babies will have heart defects, heart murmurs, genital malformations, trouble with kidney and urinary functions. The damage of FAS to the central nervous system can result in learning disabilities, short attention span, irritability in infancy, hyperactivity, and lack of coordination. Newborns from a birth mother who was heavily addicted to alcohol may experience withdrawal symptoms that can include frequent seizures.

According to the Centers for Disease Control, early diagnosis of fetal alcohol disorders and a stable nurturing home environment can go a long way to relieve the difficulties children may experience in their development. Finding the resources for early diagnosis may be difficult in some rural areas. Kinship families should begin by trying to learn all they can about FAS then inquire with local sources to find diagnosis and treatment centers. Check the local library, or online for such information. You may want to start with the Centers for Disease Control (800.311.3435 or www.cdc.gov). You can find a number of other resources on line if you search Fetal Alcohol Syndrome. See the section on Resources.

Drug Addiction Effects on Babies

Drug addiction includes legal and illegal drugs. Often a pregnant woman addicted to drugs will use a combination of substances – alcohol, nicotine, marijuana, tranquilizers, cocaine, or heroin. As noted in fetal alcohol syndrome – the drug elements cross over the placenta and reach the cells of the developing baby. Frequencies of drug use by the mother and combinations of drugs have serious effects on the baby:

- Low birth weight, premature births and the complications of premature birth.
- Drug use before birth may result in dysfunctional breathing of the infant at birth.
- Heavy drug use during pregnancy could result in withdrawal symptoms of the infant – irritability, tremor, stiffness.

A long list of other difficulties is common with drug

addicted babies.

Heroin babies usually have withdrawal within 48 hours of birth. Cocaine constricts blood vessels. The fetus that is exposed to cocaine close to birth experiences a decrease in much needed oxygen which can cause neonatal stroke.

When drug addiction is identified at the time of hospital births, the infants will be monitored for as long as four to six days with treatment during this time including a specific formula for weight gain.

Relatives who agree to take drug addicted infants will need to arrange for intensive care of a physically and mentally frustrated baby. Relative caregivers and babies that have been through this rough beginning will need a social service support system and trusted medical attachment to address possible future medical problems and learning disabilities. Critical concerns are Sudden Infant Death Syndrome (SIDS) from lack of adequate respiratory resources and infections that complicate care such as Hepatitis B and HIV. Please note: SIDS can also occur without maternal substance abuse.

Addiction is a difficult issue in our society because women who may have been victimized themselves as children carry the increased burden of blame for what happens to their babies. Grandparents and other caregivers also suffer the grief and guilt of what is perceived as weaknesses of someone in their family. Rescue in these instances require stamina and a conviction to make life for the innocent child as productive as possible. Many of the children affected by addiction while in the uterus can overcome a great deal of the handicaps and in many cases thrive on the nurturing of a loved one.

HIV/AIDS Babies

The discovery of HIV and AIDS is only about three decades old, yet the spread of this deadly disease affects millions of people worldwide and, sadly, is largely ignored by a general world population that could shift other costly priorities toward ending the terror of AIDS. Hopefully, soon, we will be able to say, "Remember that deadly disease, HIV?"

A little explanation here: HIV (human immunodeficiency) is a virus. When it enters the human fluid system it attaches itself to the disease fighting white blood cell called the T cell. Once attached the virus reproduces itself making millions of HIV virus cells that destroy other healthy cells in the body. The process of making so many destructive cells that the body weakens could take years. Research shows us that the HIV viral infection multiplies much faster in children.

When the body can no longer avoid the destructive forces of HIV making the person very sick, the infected person is identified with AIDS (acquired immunodeficiency syndrome).

Medication is available to help someone affected with HIV to stay relatively healthy and free of the sickly symptoms. However, at this writing, we know the virus continues to reproduce eventually taking the body.

The HIV infected person is still contagious. HIV is passed from one person to another *only through the passage of internal body fluids*. HIV is not passed by physical contact – hugging, holding hands, sharing a room or visitations. It is only passed through blood or sexual contact semen of a person with the HIV virus. Blood contact can come through use of syringes or unclean needles or through the birth canal of HIV infected mother to baby.

Prevention of HIV to infants: In some states all pregnant women are required to get an HIV test. All pregnant women who have even the remotest consideration that they may have the virus should get tested. Birthing a baby without passing on the HIV virus through the birth canal is possible through administration of drugs at the time of birth, but the knowledge of the mother's infection must be known.

Grandparents or other relatives who take on the care of

an HIV infected infants are eligible for medical training in the care of the baby. Specific social services assistance may also be available. The psychological burden of HIV infant care is heightened by the knowledge of the grandchild's possible early death and the grief of knowing the effects of the infection on the birth mother. The relative who accepts placement of the infected child, should also seek available therapy to help get through the emotional weight of caring for an HIV infected child.

HIV and AIDS are a world-wide problem. Though the U.S. is still in some denial which results in limited resources, a number of international resources are available to help relative caregivers. Also check the research review, *Invisible Caregivers- Older Adults Raising Children in the Wake of HIV/AIDS* by Daphne Joslin. Grandparents and other relatives facing the situation of raising an infected child should advocate with their local Health Department for services.

Effects of Domestic Violence

The numbers regarding domestic violence are devastating to any family experiencing this terrible situation. We know that women are beaten, emotionally destroyed, and killed every second of every day by someone they loved. We also know that millions of children are not only exposed to the violence of domestic attacks on their mother, but that children are also likely to be beaten and in almost 1/3 of those situations children are likely to be killed by a parent or their mother's partner. We know that most of the deaths of children during a domestic dispute are under age 10 and more than half are under two years old. We know that a few mothers are also the killers of their own children.

It is true that in a few cases of domestic assault the victim is a man and in some cases of lesbian or gay relationships physical assault experiences the same devastating affects. Children who witness violence or experience attack from a trusted adult often suffer life long consequences.

Physical assault on pregnant women is especially common in reports of domestic violence. Women suffer the emotional trauma of the abuse as well as the physical by passing on her chemical stress to the growing fetus. It is the blows to the abdomen, however, that ultimately affect the baby inside. Damage through such blows account for breaks in the placental wall, premature deliveries, and sometimes death to the infant.

Though we know domestic violence can also be a source of abuse to children, unless abuse is extended to the children, Child Protective Services may not be involved. When children are left with grandparents or other relatives because a parent is suffering abuse in the home, the care will eventually have to address the trauma the children are experiencing. This trauma may mean some form of counseling for the children.

Sexual Abuse

Children who have been sexually abused experience a horrendous sense of guilt and unworthiness whether they express these feelings or not. Children, of course, can be damaged physically by sexual abuse, but it is the emotional damage that prevails as children make their way through life.

The sexually abused child may be promiscuous or withdrawn. Girls may respond in self-destructive behavior, sometimes lasting their lifetime. They may try to prove their lack of worth by seeking out friends that will abuse them. A pattern of partnerships with someone more dominant often leads to a cycle of domestic violence. Many mothers in prison are incarcerated because they were involved as an accessory in criminal activity with a dominant man. Guess who's taking care of the children. Women who were sexually abused as children may be mentally incapable of protecting their own children who in turn may be sexually abused by one or both parents or partners.

Some boys who have been sexually abused may respond aggressively even violently to the damage of their self-image. Or boy victims may retreat into reclusive behavior which leaves them without friends or a social experience that would help them to grow into healthy men.

Sexual abuse can continue the cycle when victim becomes perpetrator. Adolescent abusers are very likely to have been victims who in turn abuse others or participate in violent activity such as fire setting. Sexual abuse, like so much other abuse, tends to stop the normal development in some children leaving an anxious young person to focus their life on self-destruction or damage to others.

Note: *These responses may or may not occur.* It is unfair to condemn a generation of victims to adult dysfunction through generalizations. Some personalities are able to overcome the psychological damages through the love and care of family. Many studies confirm that it is often one person in a child's life that can break the cycle and turn the trauma into a strength. A willingness to seek counseling when symptoms occur can go a long way to reduce the childhood damage.

Prevention of child abuse and neglect is one of the best routes to a healthy child. If abuse occurs, we know that children are amazingly resilient, but they often can not recover on their own. Children who have been damaged by abuse or neglect or sexual abuse may recover through quality counseling. Some counseling techniques show that if the perpetrator of abuse convincingly apologizes to the victim a burden of self-guilt is lifted almost immediately from the child.

Grief

When children lose one or both parents, relatives are the first to step in to care for the children. It must be remembered that relatives, too, have lost the family member and may suffer grief pain as well. The circumstances of the death can add other symptoms. If the child witnessed the death, or if the death occurred as a result of violence particularly domestic violence, children may not only experience grief from loss, but possibly a complicated array of other emotional turmoil.

Therapists agree that children and perhaps the adult members of the family may need to seek help getting through the grief. Check with mental health providers locally including the Community Mental Health Center, which may also have specific programs for children experiencing grief from loss. For financial help, look to your insurance or

---

Helping Children Through the Grief Process

Some guidelines that have been offered for working at home with children in grief include:

- Affirm children's feelings
- Be honest, don't hide information
- Get help from others
- Encourage ways for children to get relief such as a journal
- Talk about their concerns in language they can understand, talk more than once
- If, in your own grief, you feel anger or pain, model for children that getting help for yourself is important to healing
- Seek out grief support groups for children in your community
- Be patient, time will heal many responses

(see the list of other suggestions from About Our Kids at www.aboutourkids.org)

social services as a kinship care provider, or even disability through the Social Security Administration (SSA).

Check with mental health specialists on current books or online resources that may help in the healing process, such as your local hospice group (www.hospicenet.org) or About Our Kids a New York University Child Study Center (www.aboutourkids.org).

Behavioral Disorders

They come with letters – ADHD, ADD, ODD, and others yet to be identified. They stand for Attention Deficit Hyperactivity Disorder, Attention Deficit Disorder, and the scary one – Oppositional Defiant Disorder. These behavioral disorders are actual physical issues in the brain that cause the individual to require more intense involvement by caregivers including supportive therapy. Sometimes these behavioral disorders come in clusters together (called comorbidity) and in many cases medical responses are the acceptable mode of treatment.

When you look at a list of symptoms, you may identify someone in your family that you love including the child you have agreed to raise. There are warnings, however, to get more than one professional opinion on the diagnosis. In today's world with easy access to information, it is more important than ever to learn all you can about the conditions of concern. A child who is constantly trying to annoy the family or who becomes belligerent as they mature can try even the most loving soul. However, a child misdiagnosed who becomes over medicated may suffer other symptoms of distress late in life.

The point here is learn all you can about a perceived behavioral disorder and proceed cautiously on the treatment plan being sure to adjust as the years go by. Many resources exist for these behavioral disorders, see the Resource section.

Autism

Autism is a disorder that appears to parents and caregivers as "something isn't right" with their child's development. Because Autism is so prevalent, 1 in 150 children each year, according to the Centers for Disease Control, the medical profession is focusing a good deal more attention to the symptoms and the future cure than previously. Some of that research shows that a range of autism-like symptoms occur in different children. Today this is called Autism Spectrum Disorder. Some autism areas in this spectrum are Aspergers - a milder form of autism and PDD-NOS - meaning simply Pervasive Developmental Disorder Not Otherwise Specified. As of this writing, a known cause of autism has not yet been determined.

Ways that caregivers might suspect autism include a child that is unresponsive to the normal social interactions within a family, long staring at objects or into space, intense sensitivity to touch or light or colors. Early diagnosis of the disorder and establishment of a plan could help during the critical developmental stages for the child.

The National Institute of Mental Health (NIMH) is a good place to start in searching for resources on many issues regarding disorders or mental intrusions into a child's healthy development, www.nimh.nih.gov.

There is Hope

Now that you are thoroughly depressed, it is important to note that as a society we have also learned and continue to learn about ways to change the negative consequences brought on by the way we treat children with mental or physical disabilities.

We also know now that the trusting, predictable care of one person over a significant period of the child's life has been known to improve a child's self-image enough to overcome the other damaging aspects. And here's the good news for relative caregivers, some studies show that children in the care of loving relatives have a significantly higher sense of well-being than children in other types of foster care. Children in kinship care are healthier, with fewer mental problems, and less likely to have behavioral problems.

Being aware of the damage negative responses to a child's behavior or to the effects of abuse or neglect is crucial for the caregiver. Relatives can seek counseling when they understand the dynamics of the issue affecting a child's healthy mental development. They can also work closer with schools and other needs of the child on how to respond for the child's well-being.

Signs that Children May Need Professional Counseling

"Symptoms" of disease or dysfunction occur in almost everyone. How many times have we blamed Alzheimer's for normal forgetting? It is when *symptoms become a pattern in frequency* and intensity, sometimes combined with other curious responses that may indicate there is a problem. This is not to say ignore an extreme action or comment that occurs for the first time from a troubled youngster.

Counselors advise there are four areas of patterned behavior that may indicate trouble with the child's ability to progress comfortably through their development:

- **Acting Out:** When children of any age are abusive, violent, aggressive, bullying, cruel
- **Withdrawal:** Children showing signs of depression – listless, moody, unhappy, seeking to be alone, crying excessively for what seems like no reason. Refusing to talk, literally, not using words to communicate. Acting younger than their age, using excessive baby talk. Fearful – of being alone, leaving the house, sleeping, entering new adventures, or meeting new friends. Fearful of animals, bugs, darkness, Halloween, certain people.

- **Defensiveness:** Lying, cheating, manipulating others, avoiding others
- **Disorganization:** Irrational behavior, unable to recognize simple consequences –excessive losing things.

Some other warning signs that appear gradually indicating that a child may need counseling to help release a problem:

- Trouble sleeping, frequent headaches, carving on skin, bed wetting that had not been a problem before, biting nails and surrounding skin, frequent stomach aches, trouble eliminating.
- Loss of interest in friends and family or in previously enjoyed activities.
- Declining performance in school, frequently tardy or skipping school.
- Resistance in complying with rules in the family, secretive, self-isolation from others.
- Suicidal talk or especially actions that indicate self-destruction, or excessive interest in death and dying.

How to Find Counseling and Pay For It

Families who are involved with social services or public health should discuss the reasons the agency is involved with the child. If the child was placed because of child abuse or neglect or sexual abuse, counseling will probably be initiated immediately as part of the plan of care. If counseling has not been included in the care plan, relatives should inquire about accessing appropriate counseling services for the child and ways to pay for the services through the placement. Social workers and medical workers in public systems are knowledgeable about counseling resources locally and can usually recommend appropriate therapy services in the geographic area of the family. A significant amount of federal child health care dollars go for psychiatric therapy for children in placement. Some of those dollars are available for kinship care as well. Ask.

Families who suspect a child needs counseling but are not involved with public systems should check with a family physician for recommendations. Or call the local Community Mental Health system (see the section on Community Resources).

If the family has legal guardianship of the child, the family medical insurance provider may be able to recommend counseling services in the area as well as the coverage to pay for it if the child is included in the family coverage.

Another very valuable resource is a local Kinship Care Resource Center (see Section III, Community Kinship Care Resource Center). Some groups of grandparents and other relative caregivers have accessed programs that provide financial assistance for individual counseling needs of children and/or caregivers.

Questions for Counseling Service

The process for guiding a troubled individual through difficulty is based on different psychology philosophies. Some mental health therapy relies on psychoanalysis of the individual, even with a child, by addressing the root of the problem (i.e. abuse). Some therapy teaches techniques to deal with the symptoms, rather than finding the cause. Some therapy relies on medication. And some therapy sources combine techniques from all of these philosophies including the addition of medicine.

The caregiver should feel comfortable asking practical questions dealing with the counseling procedure:

The Sessions
- How often is the client expected to come to therapy sessions?
- How long are the sessions?

- Should the caregiver accompany the child in the session?
- What is the philosophy of the therapist, or treatment procedures?

Medication
- Will medication be involved, at what cost, is the medication funded under social services or insurance?
- How long will the client be expected to take medication?
- What are the side-effects of the medication?

Contact
- What is the emergency number of the therapist? If it is a general toll-free number, what can the caller expect in getting help?

There is a lot of trust involved in the counseling process. Sometimes the process can be painful. We all avoid pain wherever possible, yet in the case of mental therapy getting through the barriers of resistance could mean a life free of destructive acts. Pain is not a reason to leave a counseling experience. However, if one counselor does not seem to fit well with the situation, it is important for caregivers to try again somewhere else. To leave a counseling situation can be an intimidating process. If the caregiver sees the therapy is not fitting the need, a simple, kindly stated exit is appropriate while preparing to seek another more fitting therapist situation. Mary, a wonderful grandparent caregiver told me that it took "three tries, but we finally got a therapist that worked well with our situation."

Take Care of Yourself
Okay, time to discuss you. While the studies show that children thrive with relatives, the same studies also show that kinship caregivers suffer a long list of problems from

depression to the consequences of denying themselves their own medications. No one but other caregivers fully understands the unique stresses on the shoulders of relatives who are raising someone else's child.

Though the physical caring for yourself is imperative to your success as a kinship care provider, your own emotional well-being is just as important. You know the signs – crying frequently or getting angry easily, being excessively distracted, unable to concentrate, essentially unable to buck up to the task. It may be time to seek some professional help. Unlike the children in your care, your health insurance is more likely to cover your mental health needs. Check with your insurance company. If you are over 65 and receiving Medicare or you are receiving Social Security benefits, check on mental health therapy support through these worthy social programs.

Another valuable resource is a local Kinship Care Resource Center. Just being with others who are experiencing similar stresses can provide a great deal of relief. Do whatever you can to improve a positive outlook on life for yourself.

The self-help resources for healthy living are abundant in our society. Common sense tells us the basic ingredients:

Good nutrition, physical exercise, having fun in simple positive ways, and seeking appropriate help for problems we cannot solve alone.

School:
A Child's Full Time Job

Because School is such a dominating force on families and a partnership with families in the educational development of children, this section has two distinct parts:

- Registering and Living with *School*
- Educational support from home

Relatives who have not been involved in the life of young people for awhile then suddenly take on school age children (from toddlers to teens), are often shocked at the dominance of *School* on all their lives. From August to June, school routines and activities become a critical part of the family's life. Schools can be wonderful partners in the lives of children and they can be maddening adversaries. Whether good guys or bad guys (though our feelings are rarely just one or the other), children and caregivers are tightly woven into the school fabric, so we try to make it the best experience possible. Getting through various situations can be so much easier if we *plan ahead*.

Registering and Living with School

Most States require specific paperwork in the registration process for school enrollment such as:

- birth certificate
- proof of certain immunizations (polio, measles, etc.),
- testing results for grade level,
- and proof of authorization such as guardianship papers that show the caregiver as the official responsible party to care for the child.

Attending the Same School Under Kinship Care

If the child is attending the same school as before coming to live with grandparents or other relative, the school administration needs to know that the kinship caregiver is now the primary contact for the child. Approval for anyone else picking up the child (grandfather, older sibling, etc) should also be noted on the child's records. Because of the changes in family dynamics, schools are much more sensitive than they used to be regarding the authorized release of the children to an adult.

Grandparents and other kin should also be prepared to fill out forms that include emergency numbers, special medication or responses to the child if there is a diagnosed physical problem (if the child has asthma for example).

Attending a New School Under Kinship Care

Attending school after the trauma of being separated from a parent is tender ground for both children and their kin. To facilitate a smooth transition the following suggested process is broken into steps:

Step #1

Before taking a child to the school, find out what is required to register a student. Many school systems have registration packets that help new folks to know what paperwork they need. Don't assume that the school will let the children enter temporarily without the proper paperwork such as immunization records. Try to get what you need *before* taking the children to register.

Written authorization. When you contact the school ask specific questions particularly regarding your authority to register the child. Recent terrible events in American schools have sensitized academic leaders to develop specific entrance policies for children and their caregivers. This is a time when documented authorization is very important (see the chapter Becoming a Kinship Care Provider).

When a non-parent brings a child to school, they may be expected to have *court ordered* documentation of their authority to make decisions on behalf of the child. As noted in the legal chapter, Power of Attorney is not legally binding and so may not be acceptable in schools as proof of the caregiver to make decisions including registering the child for school. Ask what documentation of your authority to care for the child is required.

Immunization records are very important because the schools are, in most states, accountable to the State for such records. Schools could be penalized or lose valuable resources from the State if they do not comply with the records. If the children's lives have been in disarray before they come to you, you may have trouble trying to find the immunizations. If you know of the doctors, clinics, or community health department where the children received their prevention care as infants, you may be able to get copies of the records.

Previous school records may also be able to help if the children attended school in some other locale before coming to live with you. Previous schools may require that the new school make the request for student information, not the caregiver. **Academic Testing documents** will also be included in previous school records.

PR - PR means Public Relations. The initial contact with the school is a good time to develop some positive public relations. Most school personnel are very willing to help grandparents and other relatives with their part in the critical job of raising children. Keep a smile ready. Learn the school secretary's name. Ask questions with the intent of working *with* the schools. Thank everyone who helps. If an old hostility from your past begins to work its way up your system, excuse yourself for a few moments. Keep anger away from your contacts with the school. Trust me on this.

Step #2

Preparing the children for a new school. If the children come to you during the school year, arrange an after school tour with someone who can kindly show children and you around the building and answer some simple questions (save the hard questions for later – keep reading). Having a vision of the school, the classroom, the special places such as the library, lunch room, gymnasium, helps already traumatized children deal with the additional anxiety of a new school.

Step #3

Once the children are registered, get an official school calendar to post in a visual place at home. If the school calendar is just a date-list of holiday times, be sure to enter those on the family calendar. Then keep monthly notifications from the school updated on that calendar.

The school calendar is the center for families with children. Families should be sure to fill in the events regularly. Knowing ahead of time when school starts, days off, special events such as school concerts or Picture Day, PTA meetings, open house, parent/teacher conferences, holidays and meshing those events with the larger family calendar saves a lot of anxiety in the household.

In addition, the child's own classroom will have specific dated events – a science fair, a field trip, State required exam days.

Step #4

The process of getting *to* school needs attention as well. A buddy system with other children on the bus or on the walk to school can make all the difference in the child's sense of safety getting to and from school. Getting to know the families of other children in the same school is the first step to a buddy system. Neighborhood schools are great for starting such a routine. However children in the countryside or attending schools that have been distanced from the neighborhood need a little extra care in setting up the process of getting to and from school. Check with the school administration about possible "buddies" in the neighborhood or on the bus. Plan a meeting with the suggested buddy family to make arrangements for the first few days of entering school.

Now for the . . .

Hard Questions

As the child's main source of protection, kinship care providers should also learn about the school policies and process for doing things. For instance:

Lunch

- Are hot lunches served? How much are they and how are they paid (by the day, the week)? Is the child eligible for reduced or free lunch according the household income? What information is needed to apply for hot lunch services? Where do children eat?
- Are family adults welcomed to the lunchroom? Does

the school have a breakfast program for children who need to come to school early?

Curriculum

- What does the curriculum look like for the grade that the child will be in? Will the family need special resources to match the curriculum, (reference books, science material, pay for text books, if so how much, are used books available)? Is physical education (P.E.) part of the curriculum? Will the child need special equipment for P.E. (gym clothes, shoes, tennis racket, or other sport equipment)? Is band part of the curriculum? What are the sources for instruments?

Field Trips

- Does the school offer field trips as part of the curriculum? What is the process for permission to attend field trips, what are families required to sign for field trips? Is there a cost for field trips? Can families chaperone?

Special Services

- Are there special student services such as remedial reading, health services, school counselor? Does the school offer music or other performing and visual arts, or other after school programs? What is the process to access special services?

The Bus

- Will the child ride a bus to school? What are the rules on the bus? When and where is the pick up and drop off time?

What is an I.E.P.?

Ah, now there is a question. I.E.P. means Individual Educational Plan. This is a collaborative process to assist students with special needs or who may be having difficulty in school. All participants who are involved with the child's education come together to make a plan of who will do what to help the child through a defined goal of expected outcomes and to get the child through until the next I.E.P. meeting. I.E.P. meetings are often planned for children in special education programs.

Some relatives have complained that such meetings with the teacher, special teachers, diagnostic participants (hearing impaired, speech therapist), school counselor, are intimidating to the caregiver. The intention of the meeting is a wholistic approach to improving the child's school year. Caregivers are the key to drawing together the suggestions and ideas presented at the meeting in the home environment. Sounds nice, but it doesn't always work that way or even feel that way. Caregivers and children often feel a sense of prejudice against them by the professionals at the meeting. A professional leader of the meeting can set the tone of everyone working together on the child's behalf. Caregivers may want to get to know the leader (sometimes called facilitator) before the overall initial meeting. Try to keep a positive attitude and remind folks that such a plan development is for the educational health of the child.

Other programs: What are Magnet Schools or specialized curriculums? Some school systems are discovering that children learn all of their studies better when they are involved in specialized interests such as science, technical education, arts, even a Montessori approach to learning. Magnet schools, though now international, originally began as a response to breaking racial segregation barriers to quality education. Today magnet schools focus on a number of specific areas to children with special talents in an ethnically balanced setting.

Magnet schools programs exist at all levels of education. They are often schools within larger public school systems. These special programs often come under different names.

Be alert to what is happening in the school system that your children attend. Ask questions of those in authority, even if you think the questions are "dumb". If you think a program sounds good for your children, ask some of the parents how they feel about the programs before you take the steps to enroll.

Charter Schools, on the other hand, are publicly funded school systems unto themselves that have been "chartered" by a sponsoring educational source such as a university. Charter schools began as a response to public education reform offering schools of choice, one of the choices being a separate private-like school.

Volunteering at School

How can you volunteer at school? Caregivers who are able to be involved now and then in school activities through volunteer work or visits become a visible part of the child's daily life and a reminder to school personnel that this child is valued. Kinship providers who are volunteers with other parents are also good examples to other families.

An easy level in which to volunteer is in the classroom for special occasions such as parties, field trips, etc. To volunteer on a daily basis such as the lunch room or playground or crossing guard or bus aid, you may have to go through a kind of hiring process with the school system that includes a background check. Should you take a part time job at a school working with children such as a crossing guard, ask about the liability insurance coverage on part-time employees.

There are many more questions regarding school policies and events. Kinship care providers have greater success with this important phase of the child's life called school if they can follow three valuable principles:

- Know what is going on at school (and communicate activities to the family through the calendar)

- Be a part of the school environment through visits, conferences, or volunteering
- Support the child at home (see the following section)

The early days of establishing a child in school, especially a child that has recently experienced separation from their parents, are critical to the academic success of the child. Getting a good start can prevent a whole school year of trouble. School is a child's full time job. It can be a joy, a bore, or a big problem. Family Court Judges take a close look at a child's success or involvement in schools when making legal authority decisions. Much of a child's success depends on the caregiver's ability to be aware of what's ahead and be supportive of all partners involved in the child's education, especially the child.

Support the Child at Home

It may seem enough that you have had to make so many physical changes to your home to accommodate a child. You may wonder - do you have to make more room for the *stuff* that helps young students? Yes. C'mon, you know this helps to keep you alert and young. It isn't hard to academically support a child, or children, at home, and in many cases there is plenty of outside help available. The most important academic support to children at home is **Time and Space** to work.

Time

Providing Time to do homework (even when there isn't homework) is the most valuable commodity to academic success. Time applied to homework assignments includes making time for a check up from you, the caregiver. Check over math problems, writing, essays, pictures. Be careful of criticism. Children who have been separated from their parents even when the parents have been abusive, feel, as one child put it for me, "left out in space". Reviewing a child's work is a good opportunity to secure children in their own learning. Have them teach you – how the problems are done, what the essay is about, etc. If the children feel frustrated, possibly by not knowing exactly what they are supposed to be doing, you may want to help them formulate questions to the teacher or visit the teacher yourself.

When there is no homework, consider spending some time together reading (even older children like to have someone read to them) or talking about what is happening at school or making time for casual conversation about friends or dreams or concerns.

Time also means spending quality time together. Go to events at school or in the community together, watch TV or fun movies that you both can enjoy, cook together, look at family photos, tell funny stories about old relatives. Studies consistently show that the strength of positive relationships based on being together and getting to know each other significantly improves success in life. See the section on Having Fun.

Space

May simply mean the dining room table to do homework, or an actual study room in the house. Near the space should be The Tools. These can be minimal such as a drawer or box of supplies – pens, pencils, notebook paper, tape, glue, etc. Tools also include reference material (we'll get to computers later), such as age-appropriate dictionary, encyclopedia reference, history timeline. Many of these books can be purchased cheaply at used book sales. In fact, used book sales are great for all kinds of interesting books that may be helpful for younger students. So another good tool is a bookshelf near the workspace.

Computers are one of the most valuable tools any family can use. Basic tools on the computer include writing documents with the ability to make corrections easily, inserting pictures and quotes to enhance a piece of writing, using a basic encyclopedia program on the computer. Students do not have to be online (the internet) to use a computer for these basic tasks.

A good used word processing computer can be purchased at computer stores, school surplus shops, or through friends. It is best to do some research first for what you need and to get some help from someone who knows computers to go shopping with you. Or, if you can afford it, go to a good electronic store and purchase a computer for your new family's needs. (See the section on Finding Resources - Computer Basics) If you are already computer savvy, you can either share your computer with the students in your family or network their own computer with the main household hard drive.

Some Comprehensive Kinship Care Centers have a program of sharing computers with other kinship families by checking out laptops and small printers like a library book. These are a good way to get to know computers and help determine what you might need in the future.

Online

Is one of the services of computer use. It means connecting to the world wide web through a telephone line or through a cable network such as a television cable. There is a chapter in this book on basics about computers and Children in the Electronic World. For this section regarding academic support of students at home, getting online has significant positives as well as negatives. Like anything in our lives, including television, it is important to work on a balance with children. Talk openly about your concerns and the guidelines you have for bringing the outside world into your home. Learn together what can be useful and what can hurt. When the children leave you whether returning to parents or when they reach maturity, they will need to make their own decisions for their life. It is more important to teach them the process of good decision making ("What do I want to get out of this experience? What are the consequences?) than to deny them the access that they may seek somewhere else.

Other support at home includes **Planning Ahead**.

- Regular checks of the school calendar keep all family members updated and ready for big events. It's no fun to get to school with severe bed head hair only to find out it's Picture Day.
- Regular evening duties – homework done and ready, lunch money or lunch packed, any special paper returns such as (spooky music here) *The Report Card.*
- Sometimes children need special academic help that family cannot provide. Tutors are often available through the school system. Many communities have colleges or universities with students willing to offer free tutoring services. An academic enrichment business in the community may be what your student needs.
- Finally, keeping track of records for the children is critical. Many judicial decisions are influenced by how well children are doing in school. Specific current records for each child should be kept in the Important Papers file folder (See Getting Organized):
  - Report Cards
  - IEP reports with most recent date in front
  - Notes from teachers

All the extra student papers – pictures, reports, essays – should be kept in a separate file away from the critical progress items. These are generally works of love kept for refrigerators and family gifts. If, however, a student paper is recognized as evidence to some issue regarding the court concerns for the child, other actions have to be considered. If, for instance, a child reveals sexual abuse in a written school assignment, such work must be handled very carefully. There are privacy issues for the student as well as others, yet this kind of revelation cannot be ignored. In the very rare cases where a student's work identifies a problem involving a criminal act, it is best to seek legal counsel or the opinion of a therapist as to how to proceed depending on the situation.

School can be the very best therapy for children whose family life with parents has been interrupted for whatever reason. The relative caregiver that can partner with the school on the child's behalf, may find a community that supports the relative care family in immeasurable ways.

Child Care
Considerations

Wherever there are children, there are child care issues. If the children are cared for in another home or a day care facility, family concerns are safety foremost, then educational opportunities. Family concerns for child care also include schedules, money, distance to and from the care service. For kinship providers, finding affordable quality child care, whether a home care situation or educational facility, can be a horrific challenge.

Liza, a 53-year-old grandmother in a second marriage, accepted her two-year-old granddaughter, Evie, after the young parents broke up placing themselves in situations unhealthy for a toddler. Liza loved her job in a private practice doctor's office. Her husband, Jake, though very fond of Evie, was not willing to take on child care for 40-hours a week, while his wife worked. He was retired and wanted to continue the pleasured lifestyle he worked so hard to achieve. Liza began the search for quality child care only to find that the quality part of the care was very limited and much more expensive than she anticipated including a significant cost of driving distance from her home.

In spite of all that we have learned about the critical development of humans in the first three years of life, our society continues to talk about child care concerns with little action to address the issues. Some of the child care issues in the conversation are:

- the debate about mothers working at home or out in the world, a debate that continues to wear us all down and divert attention from the real child care needs of all families
- economically poor mothers who are treated devastatingly different from those who are able to choose to stay home, in some states poor mothers receiving public assistance *must* work away from home and their children
- tens of thousands of kinship care providers, grandparents especially, *are* the full time child care for their kin while parents work away from home
- child care methods vary widely from watchful babysitting to educational early childhood development programs
- lack of accessible quality child care is a situation consistently ignored by our larger national community leaving generations of children vulnerable in one of the most important development time of their lives
- costs of quality child care are so prohibitive that many caregivers experience personal financial debt or frustrating child care choices.

Let's break this down into specific topics:

- Home care – safety, development support
- Quality Day Care Facilities

- Costs and financial aid

Home care of Children

Safety: If you are caring for kinship children in your home your very first important step is to **get a medical consent form signed by the parent**. Then adjust your home for the safety of the children, especially very young children. If you are considering someone else's home care for children, you will want to make the same safety considerations.

Home child care safety should include the following:

- All delicate glassware, treasured items, and breakables out of reach and out of sight from the curious eyes of young explorers.
- All household cleaners, poisons, other chemicals and medicines put away out of sight and out of reach from children.
- Safety covers on all electric outlets.
- Safety latches or gates on stairways, upstairs windows and doors leading to dangerous heights.
- Remove or disable locks on interior doors, such as bathrooms.
- Lower the hot water temperature on the hot water heater.
- Electronic objects not intended for children should be put away.
- Appropriate safety seats for children in the car.
- Safety belts on all passengers in the car.
- In fact, car safety is a good chance to model for children – no talking on the cell phone while driving (pull over). Avoid road rage even the occasional name calling.
- Analyze the safety issues of pets in the home around children. Little children may be taught to be considerate of Fluffy, but an urge to yank hair, might illicit an unhappy response from Fluffy. Be aware of

placement of animal foods, water, wastes, and possible conditions that could cause child care problems such as fleas or skin conditions on the pet. Pet medications removed from children's vision and reach.

- Emergency plans of protection or escape in case of fire or weather disaster. An emergency plan should also include a process for contacting family.

Development Support

It isn't just babysitting any more. We know so much now about the development of the human brain and abilities of a growing little one. It is crucial to provide an environment that will help all young humans to develop skills when their timing is right. In educational terms, we used to call these *critical moments* – moments when all the neurons and accumulated data peak and the young person is *ready* to read or calculate or build or plan.

The home child care provider has a unique opportunity to enhance all this growing with experiences and tools that promote learning. This does not mean that Great Aunt Ethel has to get a degree in Early Childhood Development in order to care for a beloved nephew. It does mean that if we are able to take on the responsibility of caring for a child we are certainly able to do a few things that, at the right time, will promote the healthy growth of a young mind:

- Reading to all ages of children is one of the simplest yet most valuable tools we have. However, often there are reasons that a kinship care provider cannot read to little ones. Ways to solve this include going to public libraries that have story hours for children, buying books at used book sales, inviting older children to read to youngsters.

- Study television programming in your area and promote a few shows that may enhance positive learning. Be careful of too much TV with too little content (and too many commercials). Check www. PBS.org/Parents for comprehensive home care ideas including television programming.

- Limit any activities that demand too much time from a child denying other necessary needs critical to development. I'm talking about video games. One or two hours a day or a little more may be enough to accomplish a game challenge. Children who spend a lot of time with electronic games also need time away from the little boxes in order to grow in other areas of their lives. One grandmother told me she allows one hour of video game time for one hour of quality family time or outdoor play.

- Establish regular routines – meals and snack times, activity time, play time, nap time. Nothing, of course, is truly predictable in our world, but studies show that children develop the potential to thrive when they feel secure in their environment.

- Establish a special space for children with their own activity items – crayons, paper, child scissors, toys.

- Get some child development activity books (at those great used book sales) and enjoy some of the fun ideas together – making clay, scrapbooks from old magazines, nature hunts (even in the city), field trips to interesting safe places in the neighborhood, making easy snacks together.

- Talk with children, even the youngest ones, pointing out objects with names or while playing a simple board game. Kinship children especially need opportunities to talk out their thoughts with a trusted person.

Home care of children in today's world is a wonderful opportunity to help children to bloom intellectually. It is so much more than the limited interaction of some babysitting situations. Home care of little ones requires safety, routines, and appropriate activities for the child's healthy development. A home licensed for day care by the state does not include providing the fun of child development activities. Nor does a state endorsement assure the child's safety. Use your best information based on interviews and visits along with your intuition in choosing home-based child care for the children.

Quality Day Care Facility

If you are searching for a child care facility, you should be aware of some of the finer points in the search. There are national associations such as Child Care Aware (www. childcareaware.org) that can provide tips and referral sources for your area. The Child Care Aware website is a collaborative effort of national organizations that support quality day care and early childhood development.

Finding the right place for your situation requires some cross reference searching. First check local resource lists – the telephone book, local newspapers, advertisements in a regional parent magazine, these are usually free papers supported by advertising that offer articles and calendars on family events for the area. Then check to see if accredited child care centers in your area match programs you would like to visit.

The National Association of Child Care Resources & Referral Agencies (NACCRRA) offers a valuable "checklist" for families in their search of child care centers. Accreditation does not necessarily mean the center is right for you. The booklet "38 Questions for Parents Choosing Child Care" is available on line or by calling 1.800.424.2246. The questions are categorized covering everything including facility, safety, staff, and policies of the center.

Visits to the prospective child care center (armed with the checklist) are critical to making an informed decision. Most families will find that they have to sacrifice some of the issues that are identified with the best of early childhood development centers. The visits help families to

Quality Child Care Checklist

Following is just a sample of the 38 Questions Booklet offered by National Association of Child Care Resource and Referral Agencies NACCRRA Call Toll Free: 1-800-424-2246

Is This The Right Place For My Child?

Some Questions to Ask:

- Will my child be supervised?
- Have the adults been trained to care for children?
- Will my child be able to grow and learn?
- Are there daily or weekly activity plans available?
- Is this a safe and healthy place for my child?
- Do all of the children enrolled have the required immunizations?
- Is the program well-managed?
- Does the program have the highest level of licensing offered by the state?
- Does the program work with parents?
- Will I be welcome anytime my child is in care?

determine the priorities of their own value systems – safety, staff responses to children, predicable schedules, activities, satisfaction of children and caregivers that use the service.

Costs

The costs of child care in our country are astounding. According to NACCRRA, recent research shows that child care fees for an infant are higher than the average family spends on food. Child care for two children in 49 states is higher than the median rent cost. If the family seeking child care is working a minimum wage job, almost all of their income would go just for child care for two children in five states. No wonder families are exasperated with the search for quality child care and opt to leave little ones in very minimal care.

Child care decisions are very difficult to make. Yet for the relative caregiver working away from home, the issue is especially important.

Head Start is not a Child Care facility, though they know where one is . . .

A few words here about this wonderful childhood development program for four-year-olds and their families. As mentioned in the Community Services chapter, Head Start is a federally initiated program designed to lift little ones of low-income families into a school readiness mode that will promote academic success. Head Start programs are managed by community-based agencies, faith-based organizations, or educational resources.

Though the program can help with child care issues, Head Start is not a child care program. Rather Head Start is a family-based program with trained personnel, home-based family educators, transportation, and an integrated design where parents and caregivers play a key role in the development of the children. Finding community resources is one of the benefits of an active involved Head Start staff including child care.

The oversight process for Head Start has secured this program for decades. Follow-up studies of Head Start continue to astound new generations of policy makers with the successes of child development support to the overall health of the nation.

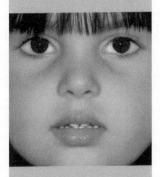

The Long Term Commitment

Financial Planning - Get a Will - Money for the Future

Children and Money

Children in Today's Electronic World

Finding Resources – Computer Basics

Don't Forget to Have Fun

Financial Planning

Let's start with the most important issue in planning for a kinship child's future:

Get A Will!

Many of the families that I have worked with over the years have so much to think about that they just can't bear to go into the issues of their own death. However, preparing a Will is really a positive step for securing relative-raised children. Children in families with elderly caregivers have the additional worry: "What will happen to me if you die?"

Families who do not have a notarized statement of their wishes after death are leaving their material goods *AND* the care of their children to "Probate" – the State authority to decide how both goods and children's care will be distributed. This is called *intestate* – dying without a will.

That sentence is in bold print because it is so important. If you were distracted while reading it, read it again. If you do not have a notarized Will expressing your wishes for the care of the children and your stuff, all the decisions will go to the State through the Probate court. Court personnel do not live with you. They do not know the subtle connections you may have with friends and relatives. They don't care at all about your stuff. Decisions by the very busy court systems in situations without a Will are based on previous experience with families you never met. The bigger the community, the more distance the court will be from your family needs.

Courts are likely to return under-age children and any funds such as insurance beneficiary or educational savings accounts to the surviving parents of the child. Children live with a relative for a reason. To place the children back into possibly vulnerable situations can be very disturbing to children who have already suffered more trauma than most of their peers.

If the surviving parent(s) are not in a position to care for the children (dead, incarcerated, parental rights terminated), the children could be placed in a Foster Care home, possibly with siblings split up. Any benefits they may have from your estate could be disposed by the State and used to pay for the expensive Foster Care system.

Kinship care guardians can prevent intestate Probate action by preparing a Will of intentions for the children and the estate.

What to Do

Talk with an attorney, kinship care support group, senior center, local AARP representative, or other legal assistance resource on how to prepare a Will that covers:

- **An executor** and *alternate executor* of the estate (even if you think you have nothing of value). The executor can be any trusted person who will follow through with your wishes as stated in the Will.

- **A designated guardian** for the children, *and alternate* in case the guardian who originally agreed is unable or unwilling to accept the responsibility.
- Specific wishes about protection of any funds that have identified the children as beneficiaries.

Be sure to follow through by *notarizing the document, make copies* and *store in a safe place.*

Back up a bit: <u>notarize</u> – when you are completely satisfied with the document go to a community notary (banks, real estate agents, local clerks office, even some grocery stores have a certified notary on staff), pay a couple of dollars and have the document notarized.

<u>Make copies</u> – keep in mind that copies are not the original, but a reference resource.

<u>Store the original in a safe place</u> – at first a Safety Deposit Box seems to be the safest place to store valuables, however some States seal the safety deposit box after the death of the holder making it more difficult for the survivors or others to get into. Check on the process in your area. Some folks put the original Will in a waterproof container and store it in the freezer section of the refrigerator (in case of fire). That sounds a little folksy. The idea is put the original copy of the Will in a safe place, then – this is important – be sure to tell a friend or relative where the Will is located. If an attorney has been hired, the Will could be entrusted to the attorney's care, be sure to check on just how such documents are stored.

<u>One more step:</u> revisit the Will at least annually or when a major event occurs that could change the intentions of the Will. A major event might be a change in financial circumstances, marriage (or loss of partner) of the kinship care provider, children becoming adults, changes in living situations of the children. Same process: if changes are made

– date, sign, notarized, store in a safe place, tell a trusted person of the updated document. The most recent date will precede any previous Will.

The American Association of Retired Persons (AARP) website provides a Self-help guide and a Will worksheet to help you get started. In addition, AARP has an association with lawyers who specialize in the legal needs of retirees including grandparent caregivers. Check www.aarp.org.

Choosing a Guardian

Naming the Guardian and alternate Guardian choices for the children requires some careful considerations. The guardian choices should be over 18 and willing to make the necessary commitment. Talk with the guardian choice and the alternate guardian before including them in a Will. Include the children in the discussion, but as guardian, you should make the best choice: someone who recognizes the time involved and possible complications of issues, someone both you and the children trust.

If the child is physically or mentally disabled, inquire with the organizations that have been working with you about available services for the child or adult in the event of your death.

Choosing an Executor of the Will

The Executor of your Will has a very special job – fulfilling your wishes in a timely manner. The Executor does not have to be an attorney, but rather someone you trust with the responsibility and with whom you have discussed your wishes – a spouse, adult child, relative, friend, or attorney. The Executor is responsible for filing your Will with the Probate Court upon your death. Then the Executor establishes a process to distribute the assets according your wishes including assuring the Guardian is ready to take the responsibility of raising the children.

Generally the process is:

1. You establish your wishes in a Will with an Executor and Guardian and alternates named.
2. Upon your death, the Executor files the Will in Probate Court to assure validity.
3. The Executor begins the process to implement the Will:
   - Notify Social Security and other resources of the death such as insurance, credit cards, and subscriptions. For many of these sources a copy of the death certificate will be required. The Executor should get several copies. A funeral administrator can help.
   - Pay debts first from the assets including taxes
   - Follow up on the Guardianship and financial Trusts for children.
   - Distribute assets according to the Will.

The implementation of the Will should be done in a timely manner. Providing some remuneration for the Executor in the Will or prepaying may help ease the burden of the tasks involved.

Living Trusts

Living trusts are a way to help your survivors to avoid probate assessment and review delays of your goods *if* you have substantial holdings – land, valuable estate treasures, or other large items that you wish to be disbursed without court intervention and costs. If you have such big-ticket items, you probably have a financial advisor as well. Be sure to discuss Living Trusts with your financial advisor before you make a Will. Our purposes here are to secure the children in your care in the event of your death.

The Living Will

Note: A Living Will is not the same as the Will designating your wishes after you die. These are two very different documents.

Statements about your care if you become debilitated and unable to care for the children should be noted in a Living Will. A Living Will or *advance directive* is a formal document that describes your wishes for your care near the end of your life.

Forms for a Living Will may be obtained from your medical professional, clinic or hospital, or from other helping sources such as Social Security Administration, AARP, Senior Services, etc.

In the Living Will you state your wishes for your medical treatment and the refusal of life-prolonging treatment when death is imminent. A Living Will is often requested in the case of impending surgery that may have complications. If you have surgery or concern for a debilitating situation that will put you into long term care, consider preparing the Living Will along with the Will of your Estate.

An option to the Living Will is to appoint a **Health Care Durable Power of Attorney,** someone you trust to make decisions about your medical treatment if you are unable to do so yourself.

Money for the Future

Getting the Will organized can be a thoughtful experience about what your dreams are for the children. Perhaps you want their lives to be better than their parents or even yours, but you wonder just what "better" means. The world seems to be so much more complex today. Is it possible to rely on ancient human values to get the new generation through a world we don't even know? We still say the words "get an education", but what does that mean today and tomorrow? The getting part seems to be the most daunting.

If the past can tell us anything, we know that the people who acquire an education in the vast world of sciences, mathematics, history, languages, human development, medicine, entertainment technology, can move in many directions, earn a good living, and be excited about the life they live.

Some kinship families are quite able to finance the education of their children, while others are still counting coins just to buy milk. There are ways, however, to support the dream with some perseverance and creative thinking. Here are a few options:

Government Savings Programs

529 Savings

In 1996, Congress authorized states to offer tax-exempt 529 college savings plans. There are two types of "529" plans offered by some states:

529 Prepaid Tuition Plans, in 19 states, guarantee tuition to be locked in at the time of enrollment for state-supported colleges. Investments are administered by the state government. A variety of plans are available from lump sum tuition payments with payroll deductions.

Anyone can contribute to the plan for the child named, which is something to consider for grandparents or older relatives involved in estate planning. The contributions are tax free at the time of withdrawal *if* the funds are used for higher education. Transfer options are available if the child does not attend college.

Questions to ask your state commission on higher education regarding the 529 Prepaid Tuition Plans:

- Does the State have a Prepaid Tuition Savings Program?
- Does the plan also cover room and board?
- What colleges are eligible for the plan?
- How are transfers of original deposits made if your designated child does not attend college?

529 College Savings Plans – Offered in 32 states, these plans do not guarantee tuition rates to be locked in.

Administered by the State government, College Savings Plans fluctuate with the investment market. There are a variety of options to invest in these programs, usually with a dollar amount limit on the annual contribution. The College Savings Plans are also tax exempt at the time of withdrawal if the funds are used for higher education.

Unlike the Prepaid Tuition programs, the College Savings Plans may be used at most colleges and universities in the United States. Check with your state's commission on higher education if such a program exists in your state. If a 529 College Savings Plan does not exist in your state you may be able to open a plan in another state that is available to non-residents.

To find a 529 plan locator in your state check The College Savings Plan Network at www.collegesavings.org an affiliate of National Association of State Treasurers.

Coverdell ESA – Educational Savings Accounts (ESA) named for Paul Coverdell, Georgia Senator, allows funds from an IRA type investment account to be withdrawn tax free when used for higher education. Contributions to the ESA of up to $2000 per child, per year, are managed through your trustee - a financial institution or investment advisor.

Gifts to Minors – the Uniform Gifts to Minors Act (UGMA), known now as Uniform Transfers to Minors Act (UTMA) allows for gifts up to $850 a year to be deposited into a child's account without being taxed and without a trust established. The donor establishes the funds in a custodial account. The custodian manages the account until the child reaches the age of maturity (18 or 21 depending on the state of residence).

The restrictions in terms of saving for education do not exist. When the child turns 18 (or 21), the money is theirs to use as they wish. Assets in the UTMA accounts are taxed by the IRS according to the minor income tax bracket beginning at age 14. The custodian of the UTMA account is a bank or an investment company.

The disadvantage of savings accounts, depending on the types, could be disqualifying the child from Financial Aid for higher education. College Financial Aid advisors weigh the student's assets more than the parents when determining need. Any form of personal savings for your children should be discussed with a trusted financial planner or attorney.

Social Security – The Social Security Administration could be one of the most valuable resources for elderly kinship care providers, especially grandparents, though inching through the restrictions is rather like playing a board game. For instance, (take a breath for this one) a child living with a retired or disabled grandparent could receive benefits in many cases if the child is not receiving benefits from a parent and the child began living with the grandparent at least a year before the month the grandparent became entitled to retirement or disability insurance benefits and the natural parent is not making regular contributions to the child's support.

These restrictions are understandable, but along with others, they must clearly fit a child's situation. Caregivers over 65 who have adopted the children have the best chance of receiving education benefits for the children. Children whose parent (or kinship care guardian) has died also have a strong chance of meeting eligibility for benefits. Children who are disabled and living with a parent or are in relative care may also be eligible for social security benefits. Some social security benefits come to a family through a particular situation. It is always best to ask a Social Security Administration advisor.

Vera began raising her granddaughter when the child was just five and Vera was 60. As a single grandmother on limited minimum wage income she thought she had no chance of getting any support for the task ahead. At the Kinship Care monthly meeting she met with the regional Social Security Administration advisor who was the main speaker for the evening. As it turned out, Vera learned that the death of her husband years before made her eligible for his social security – a substantial amount accumulated that she was not even aware was available to her.

To speak with a Social Security advisor begin by contacting the Social Security Administration:

- www.ssa.gov is a good website to explore for any questions regarding social security benefits.
- Call: **1.800.772.1213** between 7 a.m. – 7 p.m. TTY 1.800.325.0778
- Or mail:

> Social Security Administration
> Office of Public Inquiries
> Windsor Park Building
> 6401 Security Blvd.
> Baltimore, MD 21235

When writing, include as much information as possible regarding the individuals in question, including social security numbers, birth dates, address and contact numbers.

If researching online use the simplest most direct words to describe your request for example: *Prisoner Rules* offers many answers to questions regarding incarcerated family members.

Loans and Scholarships

Every high school provides a service for college bound students usually through the Counselor's Department where counselors who are familiar with the world of college money help students with Financial Aid for college.

Financial Aid is a combined package of loans and scholarships to help junior and senior high school students with the long term costs of getting a higher education.

Loans consist of student loans (Stafford and Perkins are the government funded loans usually at interest rates competitive with banks), parent loans (called Plus Loans at a higher interest and payment plan), private loans, and in some cases a means of consolidating the package at a single interest rate. Loans must be paid back. Scholarships are academic merit gifts.

Most schools are familiar with a number of scholarships including programs offered through the student's state of residence. The student who is able to research may find a number of other scholarships to apply for in their own interest areas. Some local philanthropists also offer special scholarships for children in a particular area. Scholarships are also available through organizations of caregivers or parents such as financial institutions, unions, insurances.

In recent years, folks with money who want to lift the goals of their community have offered incentives to younger children in the form of an educational grant while the students are in the early grades. It goes something like this, "I will pay for a college education for all fifth graders of my community who graduate from high school with a B or better grade average." That is a wonderful incentive. An anonymous donor in Kalamazoo, Michigan set a precedent challenge to all communities by offering a college education to *all* the students in the Kalamazoo district who graduate from high school! Such an action not only raised the level of educational value for families, it has significantly increased a positive environment throughout the community. What a gift! If your community benefactors have offered such a deal to groups of students, check with the school administration to see if your kindred children are eligible for any program.

Information on financial aid and scholarships are abundant on the internet. Just type in *financial aid for college* and you will find a number of sites offering information and "deals". On the site www.finaid.org you will find a link to a massive database of scholarships. Many of these sites are able to present information free because they have advertisers throughout the web pages. Study the information to become knowledgeable about the business of financial aid. It is prudent, however, to begin with your student's counselor at school. Attend the Financial Aid seminar sponsored by the school to get a handle on what is going on and when.

Other sources for scholarships or financial aid preparation include a family's employer or labor union. Check Union Plus Scholarship Data Base for some excellent resources on scholarships as well as writing resumes, applications, etc., http://unionplus.educationplanner.com or write American Education Services (ACS) 1200 N. 7th St. Harrisburg, PA 17102. For the big companies that offer scholarships particularly for employees, check www.collegescholarships. org/Fortune500.htm.

Students should apply for aid for college during their senior year of high school preferably before January.

Setting a goal to attend college or other institution of higher learning begins early in the student's educational career. Special interests emerge as students join extra curricular activities or excel in particular academic areas (science clubs, drama, sports) or have work experience in an area of interest such as construction jobs leading to engineering scholarships.

Actually, going to college can cost a great deal of money. Students might want to consider a Community College close to home for specialized training in areas of interest. Community colleges also offer the first two years of a four year degree to transfer to a university. Community Colleges offer excellent educational programs from Nursing (or Premed) to Forensic technology to the basic ground work for university. They are nearby where the majority of students can live at home, and they have flexible schedules for students who also maintain a job.

However your family begins the path to higher education,

the important rule is to begin early. Consider the junior and senior year job as preparing for life after high school.

Children and Money

In the previous section on Financial Planning we talked about saving money for the future. In the Children and Electronics section we barely touch on the extensive costs in the new world of acquiring and maintaining video toys. Children not only require their basic needs of shelter, nutrition, and a safe loving home, but they do live in a consumer world that is constantly pursuing young people for their life long dollars.

Many kinship families carry the extra burden of trying to raise children who are separated from their parents because of illegal family activities particularly manufacturing or trafficking illegal drugs. The view of money for these children is skewed by a tough early childhood. Teaching children about money today crosses an array of issues and values. Yet children, like the rest of us, very much need to know how some of the complexities of finances including money can have a tremendous impact on their lives.

Money does not replace loving people, the most important entity in a child's life. Teaching about money is, however, important in many ways:

- Helping children to gain work experience
- Developing a strong sense of self worth and independence
- Gaining confidence in maneuvering through money systems
- Learning to avoid pitfalls.

So how do you teach about money, especially if you have very little of it yourself? First, experts say, begin early, very early. Think about it – money is merely a means of exchange: earned tokens for goods or services. Yet the issues surrounding this simple sounding concept can be almost overwhelming if we try to think about them all at once:

- Earning money through Jobs or Entrepreneurial work
- Pricing of goods and services and ethical issues
- A myriad of savings issues – banks, investments, under the mattress
- Interest rates both for borrowing or saving
- Borrowing sources
- ATM cards
- Credit and Debit cards
- Social programs
- Taxes
- Investment in stocks, bonds, mutual funds

Whole books and teaching programs are written on just one of the above topics. In fact there is an elementary school in Chicago based on the investment concepts of money: Ariel Community Academy, an African-American mutual fund company that gives the students real money to invest as a class that is collected when students graduate, www. arialmutualfunds.com.

There are ways to help children learn about money without being overwhelmed. Ignoring the subject could leave children vulnerable to debt, frustration, poor choices. I am not an expert in the field, so this section is meant to first inspire relative caregivers to give teaching about money a good look and second to offer a few resources to help in the teaching.

Financial planning companies are beginning to realize the potential of the youth market and have responded with many designs for teaching about money. Some of those are listed here. Please know, however, that courses by for-profit companies may have other alternatives for helping you to teach children about money, mainly to invest through their company. This could be a good thing or not. It is best to use the expertise with an open mind.

Other sources come from University Extension Offices. Check the dates of the lessons. Have your children test the lessons. Share the information with your Kinship Care Resource Center.

The Federal Government also has some resources that may inspire your teaching about money efforts.

And finally, the resource list includes a few books about children and money. You may find others that are helpful to your circumstances.

Books on Teaching Children about Money

The following list of popular books on children and money is as current as I could find for you. The best way to determine if a book is appropriate for your family needs is to go to a bookstore and study the shelves on the subject. Check the publication date. The electronic world controls the world of money these days. Books published before the millennium may provide some excellent basic information in a child-friendly way. However, you will want to talk with children about credit and electronic ways to access money are also explained. Check with the big online book company for more books on the subject or to get new and used books, check with www.amazon.com.

Money Sense for Kids by Hollis Page Harman, 2005, Barron's Educational Series, 2nd Edition, ISBN - 0764128949

Raising Money Smart Kids by Janet Bodnar, 2005, (Kiplinger's Personal Finance) author is also a columnist for Kiplinger's Money Smart Kids, ISBN 1419505165

The Everything Kids Money Book by Diane Mayr,2002, Adams Media Corporation, ISBN 1580626858

The New Totally Awesome Money Book for Kids Arthur Bochner, Rose Bochner, Adriane G. Berg, Newmarket, 3rd revised, March 2007, ISBN 1557047383

Kids and Money by Jayne Pearl (Bloomberg Personal Bookshelf) 1999, ISBN 1576600645

Raising Financially Fit Kids by Joline Godfrey, 2003, Ten speed Press, ISBN 1580085369

Online Sources for Teaching Children about Money

If you go to a favorite search engine like *Google* and type key words such as *teaching children money*, you will get an astounding number of possibilities. Look for University Extension sites or family oriented sites to begin. On most sites you will be bombarded with advertising especially if you click on to a financial source such as a national banking institution.

When you click on a site you will know right away if you want to stay. If you don't, click the little square in the right corner or the back button to get you back to your search engine list. When you land on a site you want to explore but you are not sure of the sponsor of the site, look for an "About . . ." link to learn more about the site owners.

Some areas that might give you a start:

- www.extension.umn from University of Minnesota has a booklet that covers many areas of money for discussion between adults and children, "Teaching Children Money Habits for Life" by Sharon M.Danes and Tammy Dunrud. You can purchase a print version of the booklet or download it from the site.
- www.urbanext.uiuc.edu from University of Illinois Extension Office. This is a really nice site for all sorts of helpful resources on their Urban Programs Resource Network. Be sure to check with your own state university extension office for their possible information on teaching about money.

Following are just two for-profit companies listed here as good examples of financial institutions offering advice for children and money education. There are many more business resources out in the world. Check with your own financial investment resource if you have one for an educational program to help your children understand money. Go carefully over this ground. The first operative of business is Business, meaning customers.

MetLife has a series of articles assisting families through the ins and outs of public institutions including money. Their booklet, Helping Your Child Understand Money, is very basic and clear with help from the Peanuts gang:

- www.metlife.com or 1.800. MET-LIFE.
- www.moneyopolis.com from Ernst & Young is a bright site with an action game for young children to help learn about money. Many sites are available from

other financial companies.

Government resources include U.S. Government www. pueblo.gsa.gov. Federal Citizen Information Center (1.888.878.3256 or 1.888.8PUEBLO).

Working

Good old getting out there and earning money for young people is one strong lesson in what it is all about. Thomas Jefferson is credited with telling us that the work ethic is a gift that is best received before a child is 15 years of age. There is a great deal of advice in books and websites, from elderly relatives, and, sadly, street thugs on how to earn money. If your children are fortunate enough to gain some honest earning experience it may be in the best interest of the young worker to learn the 40-20-40 art of growing money: 40% for immediate needs, 20% to help others, and 40% into a growing account that may start at a puny interest, but when enough has accumulated money can be transferred to larger growing interests (check the books list or talk with a financial advisor).

When the young worker is in the job market earning a paycheck, other entities are already dividing up the paycheck. A company with employee interest or a labor union that offers significant savings and educational resources can be a real help for a young worker. Be sure to check with the Human Resources department of the company for employee benefits for savings or sponsorship for scholarships.

And of course, as mentioned earlier in the Financial Planning section check www.finaid.org for a comprehensive data base of financial planning for the future.

Children in Today's Electronic World

Let me tell you right out that the world we live in today presents us with a dilemma that grows exponentially by the month. Our children are IN the electronic world big time, whether we are with them or not. Those of us raising children today face both good and bad of the new electronic world.

The Good: The computer tools at our finger tips are incredible. No, that's too delicate a word to describe the enormity of this brave new world. Computers, cell phones, music and video tools have a tremendous impact on our lives and our children's lives. We are *living* the future. We can soar through the solar system on a satellite explorer through NASA , find the most remote piece of information, communicate with a far distant relative . . instantly, make a beautiful visual memoir, watch a movie we haven't seen in decades, listen to every kind of music from all parts of the world *as it is being performed*, play a game of chess with a friend who lives in Japan. No wonder our children are so attracted to the electronic world.

The Bad: The dilemma is that this marvelous connection to so much glorious also harbors a seething ugly underbelly of thieves and perverts and roadside bandits. We must constantly be on guard not only for ourselves, but for our beautiful children. Then, of course, other dynamics enter into it – children who have experienced family trauma and are being raised without their parents can be especially vulnerable to smooth words from predators, scammers, and cyberbullies. The very nature of adolescence presents predators with an easy target.

So what is a grandparent or aunt or cousin or older sibling raising a child to do? Avoid the electronic world altogether? Forbid it? Did I mention our human tendency toward rebellion against all things forbidden?

I once knew a charming old woman who so rejected television that she would back into the living rooms of relatives where the glowing box entertained her extended family.

Though many grandparents and other relatives are quite savvy when it comes to the electronic world, too many are still backing into the room claiming such things as being too old to learn. Though, without computer knowledge, these same tough care giving relatives will stand toe to toe with public system workers to help the children in their care. Little do they know what vast experience their children already have with information technology on other people's electronic toys.

This chapter is a humble attempt to explain some of the possibilities of the computer age, how the tools can be of value in the education of young people today. Because the dangers are so intense, warnings and resources are woven into this chapter to help protect children from the bad guys.

You may think because you are on a tight budget or limited income that you will not be faced with the children's desires for electronic toys. Whether you buy the toys or not your children will access many of them, especially through friends.

Let's break this section down by the general objects. Be sure to check the boxed side bars in this section for supportive information.

Computers

Having a computer in the home (with a printer or access to a printer) is an exceptional learning tool both for your young students and for you. Students can research, write easily (thankfully with a spelling correction), make graphs or include pictures for a presentation. The report can be stored on the computer, backed up on a CD or other portable digital device and taken to a printer. In some cases school reports may no longer require a "hard copy" (paper), but rather be shared with the teacher or class through another media format including e-mail. These are basic, easy tools that a new user can learn quickly.

Computers are also available everywhere – libraries, community centers, friend's houses. A computer in the home serves in two ways –

1. as a working tool for writing, design, data storage
2. as an online connection to the world through the internet.

Online

A home computer online, that is connected to the internet and the world wide web (that's the *www* you see on some online addresses), is a different door altogether.

Children and families can get online easily whether at the home computer or somewhere else where a computer has an online connection. The benefits are extraordinary: Instant communication with friends and relatives through e-mail, access to billions of sources of information with a click of the mouse, tuning into or sharing music and pictures. A student's report on an archeological dig in Central America can now be enhanced through direct contact with the lead archeologist. Grandparents raising a grandchild can make instant contact with a resource over a critical issue by using the internet. All of this can be accomplished after just a few minutes of learning the tool. We live in an amazing world.

Online users can set up "blogs" free. Blogs are web logs, like a diary except that it is shared with anyone in the world, though some blogs can be restricted to a specific group of users depending on the settings of the host search engine blog site. Users can develop a number of sites under different user names and different e-mails. Often the internet service provider, ISP, (normally your telephone company or cable company or through a satellite company or any number of other sources) will offer to set up several e-mail addresses as a bonus included in your communication package. You can also get e-mail addresses free from the big search engines such as Yahoo or Google. What this means is an active online user can have several "accounts" for a variety of personal needs.

This same marvelous tool, the online computer, like so many good things in our world, can become a tool for abuse.

MySpace.com, for example, as described by www. wikipedia.org/mainpage as, "a popular social networking website offering an interactive, user-submitted network of friends, personal profiles, blogs, groups, photos, music and videos internationally." MySpace is used by growing numbers of people around the world including celebrities, leaders, companies, families, children and predators. MySpace came on the scene just a few short years ago and has become a blog site of preference for many. I say this in a book, a book that takes time to print, becomes a hard copy

---

Internet Safety Websites for Kids

www.wiredsafety.org

www.isafe.org

www.esrb.org
(rating system for video games)

You can also check the websites of game boxes for parental information. Check the product box for website addresses.

---

that can only change with a new edition. In other words, here today, gone tomorrow. In the computer world, like a glamorous movie star, companies come into the scene as if they have always been here, then disappear just as quickly. Resources listed here could be out of date in just a few years, (or months, or ….).

Millions of children are sharing their dreams, their sorrow, their family history on the internet through websites like MySpace and others. With easy to set up blogs children chat together believing they are sharing with friends.

Also on these sites are predators often disguised as teenagers through their web profile. They are looking for vulnerable kids to chat with in an effort to obtain access to the family's personal information, or to get money or sex.

Scary as this may be, *to avoid the internet in your home will not prevent your youngsters from getting online.*

If your family is planning on an internet access at home through the home computer, begin addressing your concerns right away. **Talking together is the very best defense against a predator looking for a lonely youngster.**

Try to come up with guidelines that fit your family such as:

- limiting internet time,
- keeping the computer out where you can see what is happening (assuming you will have only one computer in the home),
- monitor the sites visited or designed by your children,
- and establish "parental" block programs if you think you need to do so. Remember, however, that children are very clever. They can learn intricate ways to bypass blockers.

Again, the best defense is regular open honest discussion with each other. Children should report suspicious requests from chat room "friends". This is not snitching, this is protecting other children from possible danger. Children raised by relatives often have a unique maturity in talking with loved adults. Talk about interests as well as concerns. (See the chapter on Having Fun with children.)

Wireless Computers

A home with more than one computer can be set up without a wired connection through a *router*. The computers, particularly laptops or notebooks, will need a wireless card to accept the signal from the wireless router installed on the main computer. This is tricky business. The items – router and cards – can be expensive and, unless secured, the internet access is not necessarily safe from other users within range of your signal. Check with your electronic specialists on the latest most effective wireless security if you intend to go this route. Again, talk to children about wireless use in public places, being sure that personal information is secured.

Gaming

Some international surgeons claim they learned the laser surgery skills of their trade through childhood electronic games. Electronic Games are big business today, really BIG business to the tune of *7 billion* dollars a year. Play Station, Xbox360, and Wii from Nintendo, though popular today may all be as old fashioned as the Atari years ago. Electronic game boxes are vehicles on the fast track of international gaming.

Games, in the form of small computer cards or discs, can be very expensive and easily lost. The costs may be a tool to help teach children about the economics of their electronic world. Children learn the intensity of the costs when they have to pay for the games themselves.

Games can be exceptional learning tools for problem solving, especially when the hero (the gamer) has to outwit an adversary. After all, isn't that the purpose of the ancient game of chess? However many of the video games or gaming consoles today are unreasonably violent without many redeeming values for the hero or gamer.

Rules of use, again are important in the family. Most games are identified by a rating system. Check the Entertainment Software Rating Board website for a complete explanation of the rating system and symbols, www.esrb.org. The rating symbols are easy to understand – E for everyone, E10 for children over 10 years old, T for Teens, M for Mature 17+ games may include excessive violence, language or sexual content, AO for Adults Only and RP for Rating Pending.

If the children play video games:

- Be sure to allow only age appropriate games.
- Consider placing time limits on use.
- Discuss why certain games are not acceptable in your home.
- You will want to state the rules about games for visiting children as well.

Games on the Internet (Virtual Gaming)

Many people, including children, are playing games on the internet with many other players all over the world. The game is paid for by subscription (using a credit card account). Players can enter at anytime and join the game as a team member. Players in some games can even develop a picture of themselves over their chosen character. Gamers develop personalities and physical features called Avatars and even go into business with actual expenditures and income through a credit card. One such virtual reality example is called *Second Life* where players get to reinvent their own life. Think of the psychological potential of that!

Electronic game players communicate verbally through the computer microphone (or headset) where it is not uncommon for trash-talk to rule. Remember, games are for all ages all over the world. Children could be playing the game against adults from New York to New Delhi, India. Players can even order clothing, objects related to the game and other items of interest, using the credit card, of course. Adults should be nearby when virtual games are played.

Gambling online, though illegal, is not as exciting a topic for media coverage as the other issues regarding online use by young people. But gambling addiction is a very serious concern. Recent laws impact gambling issues online. If you have concerns about gambling and the internet, check children's safety sources such as www.wiredsafety.org or other online information regarding gambling.

Music and Videos

MP3, iPod, cell phones, are as common today as the cassette tape just a few years ago. Music is downloaded to the computer through the internet (or through CDs, which are disappearing to the sadness of music makers). Though thousands of songs are free, most desired songs are "sold" to the download for a charge (again through a credit card). There are several issues here considering children and electronic music:

- though MP3's are relatively inexpensive, the more versatile iPod which today can even hold movies can be very expensive
- cell phones are becoming a source for downloading and storing the music (all using costly minutes)
- credit cards are the payment tool
- sometimes the music or movies are objectionable to your family's values

Cell Phones

Powered by towers that signal to various communications companies, then to the customer's phone, these handy little buggers are surprisingly convenient. Yes, our older generation did just fine without being attached to the phone. But cell phones have made our lives easier in many ways:

- saving countless lives in emergency situations,
- greater contact with family including elders and children,
- sending a reminder to the one who is at the grocery store to buy toilet paper.

Cell phones can be an especially valuable tool for seniors who are out in the community. Some areas even offer free or cheap 9-1-1 phones which can only be used to call the emergency number.

Cell phones, unfortunately, have not been designed for people who may have muscle disorders, visual issues, or who use hearing aids. The buttons on the key pad are close together, the screens are difficult to read, and the sound of some affects the ability for the hearing aide to work properly. These are problems that can be solved easily, however, at this writing the manufacturers and the market planners are just beginning to recognize the potential of millions of cell phone users waiting for a better tool that is not designed solely for a youth market. Check with your cell phone service provider or research cell phone products online.

It is true that our society seems to have an insatiable desire to talk for hours and in annoying situations such as driving.

Today communication companies are competing to make their cell phones the see all, do all, little electronic device. Some cell phone users can:

- take pictures
- save data using a little keyboard
- send "text" messages without an actual talking conversation
- access a Geographic Position System (GPS)
- watch movies
- write an e-mail

The possibilities, electronically speaking, are endless. Of course all of this costs money depending on the services you want. What was once a simple telephone bill has become a complicated communications bill for families.

Cell phones are purchased with contracts. Because the competition is so furious and fast changing, companies want to bind customers to them through one or two year contracts. The "deals" are based on the services, the phone capacity, the number of "minutes" purchased.

Ah, minutes. It is quite common for families to suffer the first few months' cell phone bills while young people get used to using many more very costly minutes than purchased on their "plan". Some families buy phone cards with a limited number of minutes for their children. Some prepaid phone cards can be renewed.

Dangers also exist for cell phone use. Text messaging while driving is exceptionally dangerous and is against the law in many areas. Text messaging through the internet on the cell phone can get a youngster into serious trouble by using language that invites unscrupulous characters.

Privacy is also an issue. Conversations on a cell phone can be monitored by anyone using the airwaves. It is the camera, however, that could cause problems for mischievous kids (or others who are predators). There are privacy laws in place regarding the camera on the cell phone, talk to your youngster about respect. It is not a joke to be taking inappropriate pictures and in many cases it is a felony to put them on the internet.

Loss of cell phones with valuable contact numbers is also a concern. Talk with the children whom you have allowed to have cell phones. Listen to them. Share your values and expectations. Check your phone bills regularly.

Where's the Money?

Besides the dangers of the electronic world, the next main topic of conversation for families regarding all of these devices should include cost and means of payment: The Credit Card (yipes)! Who's credit card? How is it paid? Including electronics in your family life is a great time for a basic lesson in economics.

Where continued costs to use the marvelous electronic devices are concerned – subscriptions, communications, newer software or games – purchases must include a discussion on the financial source. In my optimistic nature, I believe children want to be a part of maintaining these highly desired objects. Such a plan could well change the way children learn about their economic world. In more recent years families doled out a few dollars here and there without burdening children with the difficult issues of where the money comes from in the first place. But today, the high cost of our electronic lives almost demands that children be a part of the financial plan to support the fun.

Children are already devising their own economic plans to support their electronic desires. Birthday money launched the first games for one beloved grandson. Today he wheels and deals selling games and buying new ones all based on a practice from the ancients –bartering. He has negotiated to pay a portion of the monthly subscription to a favorite international game and no longer asks for money for electronic games.

(For more resources on other economic issues, see the section on Money and Children in the Financial Planning chapter.)

In Conclusion . . .

There is no conclusion to this huge topic of Children in the Electronic World. We are all, indeed, just beginning. Being part of this world today, cautiously, can enhance so many aspects of our lives – how we are cared for physically, how we solve so many issues in the world, how we are entertained, how we will power our big desires, how we will come so much closer together with our worldly neighbors. Everything that children (and their families) will learn today could lead to fantastic futures for all of our children.

Glossary of Online Chat

A very good service to families using the internet comes from Netlingo.com with up-to-date lists of chat texts for various groups of users. One important list is 50 chat lines parents should know. Check www.netlingo.com for learning the terms you may see on electronic messaging either on the computer or cell phone or other intercommunication person-to-person devices. Some acronyms from this new world of e-talk are even being spoken in person such as LOL which generally means Laugh out Loud or in some families it is used as a sign off for Lots of Love. Following is a brief sample of acronyms caregivers should know. Keep in mind that the acronyms change and new ones emerge. Again, talk with your youngsters about the dangers. Some of the samples below are a little scary and may mean that you need to be more aware of who your youngsters are talking to and why they are saying the things they are in this abbreviated language.

ADR	What's your address
ASL	Age/Sex/Location
BFN	Bye for now
CUL8R	See you later
CUOL	See you online
DIKU	Do I know you?
EMA	What is your e-mail address
F2F	Face to Face
FITB	Fill in the blank
G2G	Got to go
ILU or ILY	I love you
KFY	Kiss for you

KPC	Keep parents clueless
LMIRL	Let's meet in real life
MorF	Male or Femaile
MOOS	Member of the Opposite Sex
MOSS	Member of the Same Sex
NIFOC	Nude in front of the Computer
OLL	Online love
OTW	On the way – picture or document is being sent
PAW	Parents are watching
PAL	Parents are listening
P911	Parents in the room or parent alert
QT	Cutie
SorG	Straight or Gay
SPST	Same place same time
TDTM	Talk Dirty to Me
WTGP?	Want to go private – private chat room
WYCM	Will you call me
WYRN	What's your real name

Finding Resources

So much of the kinship care provider's job depends on reaching the best resource in a timely way and knowing the systems well enough to advocate for the children or the family as a whole. That is basically what this little book is all about. *Where* you find the resources is a very important beginning step.

The last section of the book titled Resources, Resources, Resources identifies key players in the job of kinship care – Health and Human Services departments, statewide Kinship Care centers, national organizations, children's organizations, dialing 2-1-1. Many of these sources include a toll free telephone number or an online internet address. The biggest risk for listing resources is that they will become out of date too soon. Grandfamilies must tune-up their awareness levels to the world around them. Some basic beginnings include:

- **Getting to know your community.** Find out what organizations that affect your family exist in the community and where are these organizations. Keep a notebook handy as you do the research. Use a telephone book, ask questions of those who are in similar experiences, ask questions of agencies that might have a connection to the area of your concern. For example, if your kinship child is having trouble in school – work with the school, but also ask school personnel about counselors in the community that may have special expertise with children, or children experiencing loss.

- **Listen to local media.** Community announcements on local radio, television, or newspapers have a great deal of information about specific programs that may help your situation. Youth organizations, Clinics, Health Department, public bulletin boards may have brochures or advertised events that seem exactly what your family needs.

- **Learn the names of people who might help you or connect you to help.** I often think of the grandmother who met a woman in the Laundromat that volunteered at a Latino Community center. The grandmother desperately needed some connection for her young grandson whose deceased Latin father was such an important part of his life. After the connection to the woman in the Laundromat the grandmother found a great range of resources for her grandson. We never know where help will be.

- **And finally, don't be afraid of computers.** If you are not already computer-wise get to know what is happening in this great list of resources. You see the addresses everywhere, the dot-com world. What follows is a guide for computer beginners.

Computers

Note: If you know computers, skip this section.

Many kinship care providers know their way around the community through visits or by telephone. Yet many folks, including grandparents, have not joined the electronic revolution. Though the peace and comfort of life without such connections is something to cherish, when it comes to getting to the best resources in a timely manner, the internet is a tremendous resource. Remember our children are already actively involved in the electronic world. There is a Buddhist proverb that fits the motivation to learn about computers, """When the student is ready, the teacher will appear". Most of the following information will not be of any value to you until you feel motivated to learn about these fascinating tools of our world.

Computer Basics

The computer is a tool to write, research, and communicate, or as the experts in computer use define these marvelous machines, " a computer is an electronic device that stores, retrieves, and processes data, and can be programmed with instructions. A computer is composed of hardware and software, and can exist in a variety of sizes and configurations." Hardware is what the body of the machine is designed to do, software is all the extra configurations including programs to write, create, or play. Then there is access to the Internet, or online with millions of other internet users.

On today's little internet excursions an online traveler can find information timely to their needs or just take a trip to the stars through the incredible images on the space exploration websites. The potential is limitless. But first you need to access some basic tools.

Public Computers

I recommend getting to know computers at a public resource

such as the local public library, the senior center, or school enrichment program. You can ask questions from gentle helpers to get you started.

One of the hardest things to learn in the beginning is the use of the mouse. This little tool is connected to the computer and shows up as an arrow, cursor (a little flashing line), or a hand to connect you to what you see on the screen.

Gently move the mouse around the pad to a spot you want to work with, stop, then with your index finger click on that spot.

Practice. It is a lot like learning to drive except that your engine is a simple usually friendly machine.

One excellent teacher of basic computer use recommends playing Solitaire on the computer to get used to using the mouse. You can find Solitaire on most computers by taking the arrow slowly to the *Start* button in the lower left corner of the screen:

1. Aim for the line that says *Programs*, click,
2. then take the curser gently to *Games*, click,
3. and then to *Solitaire*, click.

You may want to make several trips to the computer source until you feel comfortable to expand your exploration.

Buying a Computer

Computers are often sold in "packages" – the monitor (viewing screen), the main computer machine, and a printer. You will need all three parts plus *software*. Software can be purchased as CD-Roms that can easily be installed on your operating system. Software is designed to fit your hard drive.

The size of the computer is not the physical size, but rather the amount of digital stuff the computer can hold. The size of the computer includes two numbers:

- the hard drive is internal storage, holds the main operating system
- memory, or RAM (Random Access Memory) which is the amount of data you can put into the computer programs.

Computers are constructed with a few *operating systems*, however two formats of computers have emerged for the general public - mainly the PC (personal computer) and MAC (short for MacIntosh). It is not impossible, but difficult to translate between the two. PC is full of Microsoft software for writing documents, listening to music, or transferring pictures from your digital camera. MAC is easier in some areas to operate, but works best with MAC products – music (ipod), pictures, documents, filing, Mac Notebooks (small computers). Other laptops are generally PC. Though I recommend either operating system, the PC is often the reasonably priced tool with more public availability such as at libraries. So we may lean to PC talk throughout this discussion, keeping in mind that MAC is a great user-friendly computer. There are many other formats for computers. If you hear a name of another operating system and want to know more about it a terrific source of information is www. wikipedia.org where users of computers world wide help each other keep up-to-date with all sorts of information.

Software programs are amazing resources for special operations:

Word, for instance, is short for Microsoft Word – a program used to write documents, file information in folders and store documents. Most PC's come with basic programs installed:

- a document program (Word, Word Perfect, very basic Notebook and others),
- music that records and stores music for you to play or transfer to other devices,

- pictures program that allows you to put pictures in the hard drive from your digital camera and even fix them like taking out that nasty red eye,
- an encyclopedia with information and pictures that can enhance student reports.

Each time you use a program, such as Word, and save the information on the hard drive, you are using the memory of your computer to hold your information to access later.

So, first you have the computer machine – an excellent tool for working on stories and research papers especially with the help of extra learning tools in CD-Roms. You have a monitor (screen) with keyboard and mouse to select and view the hard drive programs and your data, and you have a printer to produce a *hard copy* (paper copy).

The basic computer package can cost $500 or more, but electronic stores often offer deals to help with the cost. Laptops (notebooks) cost about twice the amount of the main computer. Good electronic stores generally have knowledgeable staff that can help you with all the other details of knowing your computer, such as "burning" CD's or DVD's (recording on the discs), attaching your digital music or camera, game use, and – here it comes – going *online*.

Getting Online

Online may seem scary at first to anyone who has lived most of their life without such a worldly connection. However, once you and your family begin to use the connection to infinite information resources, you will be grateful that you allowed yourself the opportunity to enter the new world, with safety precautions.

Online means connecting to the internet via

1. the home base telephone line or
2. television cable network provider,

3. or other means such as satellite, digital subscriber line (DSL), even some cell phone services.

Public computers such as those at public libraries connect online through municipal cable systems. Some communities have even devised ways of connecting families through the school lines. If you buy a computer and want to connect at home you will need to learn about the best and most reasonable connection source in your area. There will be a monthly fee. Talk with your neighbors and electronic stores to help you decide.

Just a few online basics to get you started. This is *not* a comprehensive resource, just a starter.

You will need to subscribe with an online *service provider* – the telephone company or cable TV, or others. The cost to be online varies greatly, check for services for the price. You may want the connection added to your other service (telephone or television) and choose a separate *provider* (also by subscription) that offers better protection from the sneaks out there – a gatekeeper, so to speak. The systems of online carriers are changing considerably offering everything from packages that include free long distance telephone and 150 television channels to a simple telephone connection. Access to the internet is worth the learning. Choosing your source requires some thoughtful research.

Once online you will want an *address* for e-mail communication. An address usually has a user name (no spaces) before the symbol @ (shift above the 2 on your keyboard) followed by the service provider's name or domain name (i.e. msn, Comcast, aol, etc.) separated by the now famous "dot", ending in a *com, net, org* or other identifier. Whew. For instance, my e-mail address is <u>kincare@comcast. net</u>. When you are online and the line shows up in blue, you can simply go to the address with the arrow from your mouse, click, and it will instantly connect you. Your internet provider will assist you with choosing an address.

Browsing the Web

Key Words or Website Address

Okay, you can now connect through an internet access tool, which means you come to a *home page* flashing all the news out there in the world, advertising to you with flashy action figures and clever sounds, and giving you lots of options to "click". You will also see a search box, where you type *key words* or a phrase of information you want to know about.

For instance:

You may type Kinship Care or Grandparents Raising Grandchildren and you will come to a zillion suggested sites that have those words in the title or early in a document. If you know the online address of where you want to go, you should type that website in the very top location line, not the search box. For instance:

www.aarp.com is the website of American Association of Retired Persons that offers a ton of information to kinship care providers. The www--- should be typed into the top location line. Sometimes these start with http://. In the future the www and the http:// will no longer be used.

Kinship care on the other hand is a phrase of information, key words, that will give you a whole list of thousands of sources with the words "kinship care" in the body of the information. Type the subject or key words in the Search box.

Clicking on Websites

The websites begin with their own Home Page. Look around the Home Page for places on the site that might interest you. AARP home page, for instance, has a line of topics near the top. A click on Family will bring you to another page with a column of choices including one that says something like Grandparent Information. If you move the mouse arrow to that spot and click, you will see another "page" that also has several items that might interest you. The more you click areas of interest the deeper you will get into a site, or farther away from the site if you have clicked on a "link" that is not part of the site you were at, but rather another website resource.

Click the back arrow on the top left of the screen to go back to where you last were, you can back up several times. If the back button is light gray you should click the red corner X box on the top right to close the page.

If you type www.google.com in the address line you will get the site for a popular *search engine*. Google is so popular it has become a verb as in, "I googled Grandparents Raising Grandchildren." Search engines take key words from the *search box*, like grandparents raising grandchildren and give you thousands of sites to visit that have included those words. Other thoughts on looking at the list of sources from a search:

- Look over the site titles before you click.
- Look at the green site address under the brief basic information. If you see *uk* , the site is from the United Kingdom, *ca* is Canada, etc.
- Explore for information you can really use before you click on the site.
- Think about the best key words for searching sites.
- Be careful of your time. Libraries often limit internet use to 60 minutes or less.
- *Be patient.*

Computers and the internet can be wonderful tools. The communication, however, depends not only on the machines with their own computer programming language, but also on the humans who input billions of pieces of information into the research devices.

Though the speed of information is truly astounding, we become so used to "high speed", our impatience sometimes gets in the way if we want the choices to come faster.

Libraries charge for page printouts. Think carefully about all the interesting things you want to copy.

If you allow yourself to practice browsing, you will learn so many things about the unique computer tool and its potential.

About the Bad Stuff

When we think about connecting to The World, we have to realize that 80% is generally interesting. 10% is downright lovely. But then there is that minority of scum that have learned the tool as well. Instead of standing at our door purporting the benefits of snake oil with their hand out or surveying our environment for a heist later in the night, they are waiting for us to cruise by innocently on the internet.

There are some basic rules that everyone should consider:

- Never give personal information to anyone you do not know or that you do not intend to have your personal information, especially credit cards, bank numbers, social security numbers. If someone you "know" contacts you by e-mail (you didn't contact them), like your bank, to say they are having a little trouble and they need you to verify your personal numbers, do not click on the site, if you do click the e-mail and recognize a possible scam, delete it and contact your bank or credit card source to let them know someone has copied the look of their site in a possible scam.
- If you order things online, check with the seller for their safety measures that the seller should have to protect your personal information.
- Be sure your computer has internet safety applications or software against "virus'" and "spyware". Your provider or electronic seller should help you with

these protections.

- When you go to various sites a "cookie" is often attached to your internet HTTP source that tells the site that you visited, who you are and that you are interested in them. Then they will likely send you advertisements. Check with your provider on how to clean "cookies" off of your computer regularly. It is easy and one of the many subtle things you will learn like driving a car.

Establish computer use and safety rules with the children in your home (see the section on Children in the Electronic World).

Well there you have it, a very skimpy beginning. I hesitated to even put this chapter in the book, except that more than a small minority of kinship folks that I have known, have little or no knowledge of the vast computer world impacting all our lives. The power of the electronic world does require us to have at least a working knowledge of the influences on our young ones.

Don't Forget to Have Fun

While in the sorrowful work of developing a child abuse prevention program, I learned something very important about child development: there are at least two sides to every life. Children may suffer significant assaults on their growing self-image – degradation, beatings, sexual intimidation, loss of a loving adult – all of which may need vigorous therapy to repair, but sometimes the best therapy is a change of direction. I once heard a young actor, Robert, describing his childhood in a rough urban neighborhood. He was wooed by the badies just because he was there and that was the most dominant recruitment on the block. One day another boy in the apartment building was running off to catch a bus. "Where are you going?" Robert asked.

"To drama class. It's great. Come with me." He went just for something to do and was hooked. Today the actor is certain that if he had gone for the close at hand entertainment of hustling little old ladies he would be in prison now. The point is that we focus so much on the "problems" in ours and our children's lives that we forget to have fun, and possibly change the whole direction of our lives.

Communities today are filled with a wide variety of activities for families and children to enjoy and learn about new worlds all around us. If something of interest doesn't take hold in one of these programs, families can make their own path to having fun.

A few years ago an important family life study emphasized this enlightenment for me. Instead of looking at what's wrong with families struggling with trouble, the study found a few common factors showing up in successful families (families that stick together, raise children that overcome adversity and thrive into adulthood). Some of the factors they found are:

1. Affirmation – family members affirmed each other's presence regularly with a smile or small gestures that showed they were important to the family, giving general personal support.
2. Clear expectations – adults in the family identified reasonable expectations for maintaining a supportive household from regular chores to expected conduct outside the home.
3. A process for solving problems – the families worked together to solve problems either through family meetings or regular respectful discussions.
4. Did interesting things together – the families traveled, took classes, talked, generally they developed ways to enjoy each other.
5. Tell family stories – keeping family history alive even when some of the stories were sad.
6. Seek help – when there was trouble these families reached out to the community of services to get the help they needed.

Hmm, doing interesting things together and telling family stories. That's one way to have fun. How many dreams have we adults had that were put aside because the urgency of the moment required our attention. Kinship care providers often feel like they are walking swiftly over a long path of hot coals. There is no time, some say, for family enjoyment. Yet as any grandparent or sister or close relative knows very well: worry is exhausting. Sometimes we can't rush the speed of court dates or social services decisions or the long hoped-for change in an adult child or any number of other big issues constantly on our minds. You are nodding, I can see it. Let's have some fun here. Are you ready to tell your good stories of so many interesting things in your own lives?

☐ Telling family stories leads to the great adventure of exploring your own family through *genealogy research.* Bring the children along. Use the internet. Go to libraries. Take little snack breaks to talk about what you are finding. Develop a filing system. For some this type of family history brings the history of all of us into focus. We find some stories that are sad, some are funny, and we find old family members that connect us to major events in the world.

☐ Americans (maybe most cultures) are collectors. These interests can lead to a lifetime of specialty knowledge from sport memorabilia to the smallest curious items. The search for these collectibles can take us to fascinating places and meet some very interesting people.

☐ Maybe its studying history itself, or natural wonders, or specialty places that stirs the imagination. If you don't know what adventures are around you, try this: make a 60 mile circle on a map with your home area as the center. All the little towns or neighborhoods in that circle have some great places to visit or stories to tell – zoos, museums, sporting events, nature centers, beaches, parks, specialty shopping, etc. What are some of the day trips in your area that could be fun to visit? If 60 miles is too far, try your own home area. Once we start to look about us we find a world of things we never knew existed.

☐ If you are part of a strong ethnic culture, you and the children could research the heroes of your ancestors – make a scrapbook or a brief biography book of what you find. Children develop a sense of pride once they become aware of the folks in their cultural heritage who have made a positive impact on our human adventure through history.

☐ Community programs offering lessons in art, sports, writing, building, drama, sciences from nature to rockets, are often offered through local recreation or organization programs. Sometimes these are called camps. Though some of these programs cost money for a one day to a six week period, scholarships or sponsors may also be available.

☐ Volumes of books have been written on home activities for families from making scrapbooks to making bread. Learning to cook is one wonderful thing to do together. Yes, there is sometimes a mess. Messes can be easily cleaned. The opportunity to create with a loved adult – talking together the whole time – then sharing the creation is a gift that lasts a lifetime.

When Carlos came to live with his Aunt Nita he felt angry and frustrated by the events in his young life that he thought made him different from other kids. The new therapist suggested to Nita that they try to get Carlos a Big Brother. Enter Javier. When Javier first met Carlos, the boy's resentment had turned to aggressiveness. Undaunted Javier stayed steady with Carlos taking him to a variety of sporting events, trying to play basketball with him, but the good intentions barely dented the wall Carlos built around himself. Their relationship changed from indifference to curiosity when Javier showed Carlos pictures of Javier's own unusual family of adopted brothers and sisters from many ethnic backgrounds and regions. But the real change came when Javier brought out the baseball card collection. The two began a quest for baseball card treasures that took them all over the city visiting stores and talking with other collectors. Carlos and Javier remained friends as adults when Carlos worked his way through college in part by selling some of his valuable collected sports cards.

Many famous people found their career nitch through an interest developed when they were a youngster. Steven Spielberg was making movies by the time he was 15. Wilma Rudolph (look her up, it's a great story) ran for her life when she was just a little one then went on stun the world with an Olympic victory.

So, *don't forget to have fun* – here is a mix of ideas and resources to kindle your spark.

- Visit local universities or colleges art or natural sciences departments.
- Write a script and make a movie or a commercial. Take a class in movie making or attend a Children's Film Festival.
- Make ice cream with variations, how about lemon drop crunch?
- Talk with re-enactors – or join one. These events re-enacting history are happening all over the country – Civil War, French Explorers.
- Collect postcards of people and write stories about them. Around 1900 the postcard was like the e-mail of today. Photographers would travel the countryside and take pictures of the customer to put on a postcard. The faces and styles and the way people posed are great material for telling a story.
- Make a family newsletter with pictures. You can use the computer or old fashioned paper, pen and glue.

- Grow vegetables or flowers. Not always seasonal. In the middle of winter you can grow a sweet potato in water or an avocado seed, or plant orange or grapefruit seeds – they grow into beautiful plants.
- Visit a local violin maker or a wood carver or an artist.
- Visit a diary farm – recycling center – or big rig truck depot. All of these places play a big part in our lives. Visiting them opens whole new worlds of knowledge.
- Read together (there are some wonderful books out there). Check out *Missing May* by Cynthia Rylant for helping a family deal with loss.
- Just tell stories – tell a progressive story – one person starts and others add to it until its done.
- Organize family photos. Most of us have boxes of photo packs that need a good going through. For children with recent loss, this could be a sensitive experience, proceed cautiously.
- Go to a pet show. Cats, dogs, horses all have a big market of interested owners.
- Join a charitable organization that addresses a special need such as the local humane society.
- Watch a movie and talk about what was good or bad about the movie. Watch to the end where the credits roll by. Talk about the production team's work.
- Stay up late and go to a local Observatory for a view of the night skies through telescopes.

This is just a small list of fun things to do. Having fun with the family is often the best defender in the choices children make as they progress through their developmental stages. Too many children choose gangs that are involved in criminal activities because the children have a desperate need to belong to a group (a family) that accepts them. Kinship children need to know there are choices in their future that can make the difference between a drug deal gone bad, or flourishing in the embrace of a family that shows them positive choices in their life ahead.

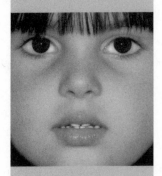

The Community Kinship Care Resource Center

Types of Kinship Care Support Programs

Establishing a *Comprehensive* Kinship Care Program

Types of Community
Kinship Care
Support Programs

The City of Detroit has 17,000 kinship care families. Seventeen *thousand*. These folks not only take on the parenting responsibilities of a relative's children, they also enter into a web of social services or legal entities related to the new family situation. Kinship care providers, as you have read, brave elements that parent-child families rarely have to face all at once: Childhood trauma, challenging public systems, dissension in the family, extra hidden expenses, and legal entanglements related to the cause of the kinship care.

Detroit is not unique in the growing needs of Kinship Care families. According to the U.S. Census 2000 (almost a decade old):

- Chicago has 41,328 kinship care families,
- Los Angeles, 30,511
- Houston, 25,347

- Philadelphia, 21,123
- New York City, an astounding 83,949 kinship care families, more than the entire state of Michigan.

In the small towns of Middle America and in the rural outskirts of every state – grandparents, aunts, uncles, older brothers and sisters, distant relatives, friends, neighbors, are raising somebody else's children, *millions of children.* (See the populations by state in the Resources section.)

Families trying to secure their new kinship life, working on the most immediate physical and psychological needs, do so much better with the support of caring communities.

Without community support, kinship families are isolated, children may be shuffled through independent services causing excessive travel, appointments, and record-keeping. Without community support, children are at greater risk of growing up with limited education, without goals, carrying unresolved emotional baggage into their adult lives that interfere with their positive quality of life and potential as a citizen.

With community support, kinship families are embraced, children and kinship care providers become enriched partners in developing healthy communities for the future.

Supporting the grandparent kinship care provider - (in many cases the great-grandparent) raising grandchildren, also means communities addressing the special needs of seniors who courageously assume the responsibility to raise healthy-minded children.

The goal of kinship care, as we have stated many ways, is to raise healthy secure children who can reach a maximum potential for themselves and their community. This is not just a goody-goody cause. Kinship care providers save the larger community – States and the Federal government – immeasurable sums of money in residential care of children alone. We don't even talk about the savings decades later when the children grow up healthy and become productive citizens.

Types of Kinship Care Programs

A community that openly cares and supports kinship families can help best with easily accessible centralized Kinship Care Programs. Kinship Care Programs can address the unique needs of grandfamilies and especially in filling gaps with other community helping services.

Kinship Care Programs come in all varieties. The programs may simply be a gathering of kinship care providers to share common problems and solutions. Or, to be more effective, the programs may be more comprehensive, strengthened by the unified efforts of the larger community. Programs may include one or all of the following elements:

- regular support group meeting under the guidance of a therapist, with safe child care available
- family informational meetings with community programs, possible evening meals provided (groups work better together when they eat together)
- a four or six-week curriculum course covering specific kinship care issues
- casual get-togethers after the curriculum course
- in-home, one-on-one consultations of the family's needs with an advocate knowledgeable in kinship care issues
- legal assistance
- personal therapy assistance
- assistance with social services programs
- a 24-hour call line or other communication such as websites with chat support between families

Some community supported Kinship Care Programs can even offer special conferences for providers and day camp for children.

The groups have many different names – Grandparents

Raising Grandchildren (GRG), Grandparents As Parents (GAP), Relatives As Parents Program (RAPP), Second-time Around, Kinship Caregivers, Grandparents Resource Center (GRC), and one of my favorite group titles from Battle Creek, Michigan – KIDS - Kinship Is Divine Strength.

Though the programs vary from the basic get-together to a whole list of services, it is the *comprehensive* Community Kinship Care Program that can impact more complete services to families. Comprehensive Community Kinship Care programs can even develop clout on the policies and legislation that govern services. This chapter will discuss all types of community kinship care programs from the basic programs started by kinship care providers to setting up a comprehensive Community Kinship Care program that provides a multitude of services.

Starting a Neighborhood Kinship Care Group

Almost every grandparent raising a grandchild tells how alone they've felt with the big issues of raising their grandchildren. It is not until they meet up with other relatives in the same situation that they realize they are not alone. There are many kinship families in their own community trying to make their way in our complex world with very little help.

Following are ways to establish types of kinship care family groups beginning with the very basic, The Meet Up, to developing a strong organization with paid coordinator and funds for services.

The Meet Up

Relatives who want to find others in kinship families just to talk about their common concerns should begin with an initial outreach. Announcing such a meeting could bring a lot of participants, in fact, with the right notification, I would almost guarantee that several families could show up. Here's are simple steps to start:

Types of Kinship Care Programs
The Meet Up
Casual get-together
The Support Group
Therapist available for psychological issues
Regular Meetings
Regular meetings with speakers from community
Comprehensive Resource Center
Full service program with strong community support to help individual families and offer regular meetings

- Plan a time and place to meet – coffee shop, school, church, senior center
- Advertise in the neighborhood with posters, at social services, health department, doctors, schools, the places kin families frequent; send a little news announcement with information about the meet up to local media (include who, what where, when)
- Arrange *safe* child care in close proximity to the gathering
- Arrange simple snacks if the place is a public service building.

Regular Meetings

Once a Meet Up group begins gathering and learning about their concerns and joys, providers may want to take the next step to organize a bit further by planning *regular* meeting times and place. They may want to arrange a speaker on a common subject - social services, legal issues, psychological issues, health concerns, school issues. Many organizations offer knowledgeable speakers for free, just ask. Again, be sure to arrange outreach, safe child care, and snacks.

Therapy Support Group

Some agencies, like a senior center, began kinship care groups with a hired psychologist to host regular therapy support groups. The meetings are arranged by the agency. They may provide child care and snacks. The main idea is to offer a time for kinship care providers to address issues that are disrupting the home environment – a sleepless child, grief, aggressiveness, fear of drug use, behavioral conditions. Often a Comprehensive Kinship Care program will emerge from the Support Group process.

The Comprehensive Kinship Care Program

Our nation is filled with like-minded groups gathering in Meet Ups or Regular meetings, sharing information, helping each other on the sometimes difficult road of kinship care. Eventually, like the families themselves, security of the group begins to take hold and the need to become a Comprehensive Kinship Care program becomes necessary.

Just what is a Comprehensive Kinship Care program? Groups that meet and gather information or for psychological support often find themselves severely limited when dealing with the *other* services kinship providers may require. They often need information and assistance with health care, financial aid, legal issues, or individual counseling.

Small groups meeting also find that they are only reaching families who are willing to share their concerns. Many families desperately need help but are unwilling to join a group or even discuss their issues with others. A funded Comprehensive Kinship Care Program can serve both families that support each other in group meetings and families who are less willing or able to attend such meetings.

A Comprehensive Kinship Care program can offer a variety of services:

• One-on-one consultation from a program advocate

with the kinship care provider to assess the family needs
- Guidance and support with community resources
- Assistance to establish legal, counseling, and other professional support
- Regular get-togethers for social contact and information on the specific issues
- Regional conferences with other area community groups
- Community education
- Funding for these special programs

Establishing a
Comprehensive
Kinship Care Program

"I heard an interview on the local radio," Sally, a 66-year-old grandmother, described her first encounter with the Kinship Care Program in her community. *"So I went to the meeting that night. I was a little nervous. I didn't want a lot of sympathy. I just wanted to hear the speaker on doing taxes for grandparents raising grandchildren. They said they had child care so I brought my 8-year-old grandson, James.*

"On the way home," Sally added, *"I asked James what he thought. He smiled and said it was fun. But the best part was being with other kids living with their grandparents. 'I thought I was the only one,' he said."*

How a Comprehensive Kinship Care Program Operates

A Comprehensive Kinship Care program depends on an active, knowledgeable Coordinator. The Coordinator has two main jobs - to serve the families (or supervise a staff of advocates) and to make sure the community knows why this group exists and needs community support. Think of the following as a job description of sorts for kinship care coordination and staff.

The Coordinator for a Comprehensive Kinship Care program manages the overall program to strengthen kinship care and improve the efforts of these special families.

The Kinship Care Program should:

I. Advocate for Families:
- Establish regular informational and or support meetings.
  - Including quality, safe, activity-oriented child care.
  - Advertising the meetings.
  - Securing appropriate speakers.
  - Arranging for refreshments.
- Meet with and assess the needs one-on-one with the individual families.
  - Listening to concerns and noting the specific services required: legal counsel, financial assistance, therapy.
  - Develop an action plan for the kinship care provider.
  - Be available for follow-through or even go with the families to the various agencies (which can sometimes be intimidating to kinship care providers)

Note: A good Kinship Care advocate respects the privacy of the families and the confidentiality of the family involved within the public systems. The advocate knows how the public systems work and helps to prepare families for the initial experiences. A Kinship Care advocate is prepared to be available for families and prepared to leave confident families to their own new knowledge.

II. Develop Community Strength:
- Educate the community about kinship care issues through local media, service club talks, news releases
- Advance communications within the group through newsletters, buddy system, telephone and website
- Collaborate with other human service agencies to merge services or to improve services to kinship care families such as housing and transportation
- Collaborate with other Kinship Care programs in a geographical region to expand information and services (such as an annual conference)
- Secure agreements with special assistance services to families such as legal counsel or therapy

III. Maintain the Program:
- Secure funding to strengthen the program through grants, fundraisers, and other coordinated community funding (such as United Way)
- Prepare regular reports on the progress of the program for the Board of Directors, the parent organization, and funding sources
- Establish and facilitate meetings of an Advisory Board of Kinship Care providers that help to address the needs of the local organization and its participants

This program description may seem daunting, but such work is being done all over the country with the support of senior oriented organizations such as Area Agency on Aging, Office of Aging Services, collaborative human services, YMCA's, State University Extension programs, or local Senior organizations such as AARP.

The benefits of a Comprehensive Kinship Care program are especially felt when children grow up healthy and goal oriented, knowing they have been loved enough to gain the security of their family *and* their community.

How to Get a Comprehensive Kinship Care Program in Your Community

There are two ways to secure and expand a kinship care group into a Comprehensive Kinship Care program:

1. Join an established non-profit organization such as a Family Services organization, Senior Services Center, YMCA, or other appropriate group as one of the programs under the umbrella of that group.
2. Become an independent non-profit organization with a board of directors, accountable officers, and viable financial plan.

1. Joining an Established Non-Profit Organization

A small kinship care group that wants to expand programs should consider these questions:

- Are other small kinship groups meeting in the wider community (in faith-based centers, outlying communities, etc)?
- Does a centralized comprehensive program exist in the area serving a large urban center and a wide ranging rural surrounding? If so, how is a satellite program brought into the fold?
- Does a local university offer organizing resources?
- Does the state have a centralized Kinship Care Resource contact? (See the Resources section.)

Answers to these questions can help a small group to determine the direction they want to go to establish a more comprehensive kinship care program.

If the community does not have a Comprehensive Kinship Care program, active kinship care providers can generate some interest with an appropriate family-oriented organization. Some organizations may have already had some interest either from their national organization or

Two Ways to Develop a Comprehensive Kinship Care Resource Center	
Join a Non-Profit Organization	**Become an Independent Organization**
Senior Center, YMCA, Family Center	File for Non-Profit, Set up Board of Directors, By-Laws, Fundraising Plan
Seek funding to supplement the parent organization support	Write grants, do fundraising

from local members. Federally funded aging resources, for instance, have encouraged local organizations to address the needs of grandparents raising grandchildren. An active local AARP is very familiar with the needs of kinship care providers and may be an important initial resource.

If an established non-profit organization such as a Senior Center wants the job of sponsoring or including Kinship Care in their programming, they already have one of the biggest steps taken care of: the *501(c)(3) federal tax deduction for non-profits*. Having Federal non-profit status means that the organization can apply for funding through grants or other resources to help accomplish the goal of hiring a Coordinator to design and secure the Kinship Care program. The organization can also obtain other funding for specific parts of the program as well as conduct fundraising for general support.

How to Find a Non-Profit Organization Friendly to Kinship Care

Before approaching an organization, kinship care providers that have been meeting casually should get together for a *vision* discussion. Plan a comfortable meeting where members can talk freely about the possibilities and needs of a comprehensive kinship care program. Ask each other questions that address the needs of the families:

- What do we as kinship care providers and families need most? This is where everyone loosens up. After the funny comments, dig in with some real concerns – financial help? Therapy help? Legal support? Reaching out to other families? A paid leader to get things done? Someone should be writing down all the items for identifying priorities in the vision.
- What do the children need?
- Does our community have an active Senior Center, AARP, YMCA, Family Services Organization, or State University Extension Office? Who is the director of the organization? What are the contact numbers?
- Where are other Comprehensive Kinship programs in our geographic region?

As the questions and answers flow, a vision begins to develop of the possible new program. Members of the group should plan visits to communities that have developed kinship programs to get an idea of what is working and how their own community may adapt to local needs. If possible, go on-line and "visit" other programs that look successful. E-mail the personnel of successful programs for any help. Sadly, you will find there are a few superior programs and a lot that started out enthusiastically, but barely exist now. Stick with the successful folks and learn all you can. See the Resources section for statewide kinship care resources – ask for a contact list of programs in the state.

Once the ideas about the vision for the program become clearer, the group should prepare a *vision statement* that includes a list of needs that could be fulfilled by a comprehensive program. For example:

The Brewer County Kinship Care Resource Center supports grandparents raising grandchildren and other non-parent relatives raising children through a variety of programs including community education, public systems support, and socialization funded through grants and community support.

This is just a sample. The development of the vision statement should be carefully studied by those who are invested in the development of the program. If possible, include some suggestions on funding sources based on the group's research. Once a vision has been sketched out, the chosen organization can be approached.

Prepare a "proposal" to leave with the intended organization that includes:

- summary of the research from your visits to other organizations
- numbers (use the U.S. Census data on kinship care, any other data support regionally and locally)
- a very general outline of the possible work of the program, "We see the kinship care program managed by a coordinator and staff that will work one-on-one with families, organize monthly meetings, seek funding to support the program, work with agencies on behalf of kinship care providers in our community."
- a very general budget of the main line expected costs, "Based on our research, we expect the total cost of the program to be about $.... to cover the hiring of a Coordinator and address the specific needs of kinship care providers."
- a list of individual leadership in your group and contact numbers of those that can testify to the need for a kinship care group
- a cover letter that expresses gratitude for the meeting and an expected date of response, (suggest a reasonable time – a month, two months so that the leadership can address the request with a Board of Directors and other advisors to the organization).

Arrange a meeting between the leadership of the proposed organization and two or more members of the kinship care group.

With a well prepared proposal and a positive meeting of intent, you might expect the organization to request a presentation at the Board meeting as well.

Often this initial beginning will set the wheels in motion so fast that in just a few months a viable Comprehensive Kinship Care program can be up and running.

2. Become an Independent Non-Profit Organization

The big issue for an independent program is trying to get enough funding. An independent organization that has developed a Comprehensive Kinship Care program is an option that should be considered when an appropriate existing parent organization is not a solution.

Once again, imaging is an important first step (see the vision development above) – what do we want out of this program? How can we get it? Take all the steps of developing the vision described above. When a clear picture of the program is agreed upon by the organizing members it is time to take the actual organizing steps. Hang on – this takes some real commitment.

The Steps to Becoming a Non-Profit Organization:

1. **Set up a Board of Directors** – this can be 3, 5 or whatever number. Manageable and odd number of board members is better for vote and meeting purposes. Decide on a Name for the organization. Oddly, choosing a name seems to be one of the hardest parts of organizing because the name cannot be the same as other organizations, yet the name must mean something to the people who search out the organization. Sometimes a similar name with a geographic location included can be enough to distinguish the program – for example, Relative

Caregivers of Clearwater County.

2. **Decide what it is you intend to do as an organization** – sometimes called a mission statement. This is usually a one or two line concise and clear statement, "the Relative Caregivers of Clearwater County will assist and support non-parent relatives raising related children . . ." Choose the words that all founding members agree to and could state easily if asked.

3. **Elect "officers"** – a President, (director, head honcho), a vice President that will act as leader in the absence of the President, a secretary that takes notes and records them for all members, and a financially astute Treasurer (not just a guy with a computer program). Some accounting firms are willing to commit to community service allowing one of their accountants to serve on the board.

4. **Non-Profit Corporation:** With mission statement, first board meeting and officers named, the next step is to apply for Non-profit Corporation status at the commerce division of your state. Every state process for filing as a corporation is different. You may even apply online using a credit card. The form may need to be signed by the officers. Fill in the areas that are needed for this important step. Expect the filing process to take some time. Some groups report a month or more. There may be a small cost, (or a big one $20 to $200)

5. **Not done yet - the 501(c)(3).** Once the organization has become incorporated it is time to file with the Federal Government for the 501(c)(3). This form can be obtained through the U.S. Treasury Department or on-line at www.usa.gov (800-333-4636 or 800 Fed Info) or check with a local lawyer. The form is long and testy, requesting in many ways just what you want to do and how you will do it. Just be clear about what it is the organization is about and how the business will be

conducted - paid coordinator who is responsible to the Board of Directors to implement approved activities and goals of the organization; goals and activities include . . .(see the following sections on developing a Comprehensive Kinship Care Program).

While waiting for all the non-profit incorporation papers to be approved the group should continue meeting to decide on a plan of action with goals and how goals are going to be accomplished – namely – develop by-laws and a budget. Check with other similar family oriented organizations for workable by-laws or check books on the subject.

What About the Money
Once the organization becomes a Comprehensive Kinship Care program, either under a larger non-profit or an independent viable non-profit tax deductible group, the FUNding begins. This is when being a part of an umbrella organization may be more helpful than small private groups going it alone.

A note about a hired coordinator: Though it seems benevolent to have someone volunteer to lead the group ("think of all the money we'll save"), having a paid coordinator position means accountability and seriousness. Hiring someone who not only wants to do the right thing by kinship care providers and their children, but *knows* the helping systems involved and how to deal with them can greatly improve the survival rate of a new organization. A hired coordinator should be someone who understands public budgets and the process for accountability to the Board (or umbrella organization). Volunteer leaders with all good intentions and knowledge still burn out from the enormity of the tasks involved, which too often leads to the end of the program.

Kinship Care groups are dealing with very sensitive issues. It is critical to have someone who understands confidentiality and liability. One way to find a qualified coordinator is to seek out dedicated and experienced human services workers in your area. A clear design of the program needs should be presented to prospective candidates and a defined job description.

Finding such a coordinator is not as hard as it sounds. There are many dedicated human service professionals available in communities, some who are even raising a kindred child, though that should not be a criteria for hiring.

The paid Coordinator of the Comprehensive Kinship Care Program is the largest piece of a very small budget pie, about 2/3rds of the budget. Warning - the following is probably going to date this little guide book considerably, but we have to talk about numbers, so here goes.

A really comprehensive program serving approximately 40-50 families can operate on a skeleton $30,000 to $40,000 a year. The Coordinator cost includes a part-time worker (about 30 hours a week). An umbrella organization may choose to hire a professional as on-staff personnel under the guidelines of their organization. The budget also includes funds for special assistance in legal and therapy services, child care, supplies, communication, and discretionary funds (money to support urgent needs for the families). All of these categories are discussed later in this chapter. As the numbers of families increases, so does the time and responsibility of the coordinator especially as more staff may be hired. With growth comes an increase in the budget.

Independent non-profit organizations may consider hiring the Coordinator as a contracted position. Some organization designers feel that contracting services is not really fair to professional personnel – it generally means the Coordinator is self-employed, responsible for their own taxes, liability insurance, etc.

The organization services should always be free to the families – no dues or subscriptions. A strong kinship

---

**Comprehensive Kinship Care Center
Sample Budget**

The following budget is a *sample*. It may appear high to you or low, or inappropriate in some areas. However you view this sample budget, please keep in mind that it is meant to be a general measure to design a community kinship care center. A $50,000 budget to manage a comprehensive *full service* kinship care program is doable in mid-size communities with a combination of funding sources.

Coordinator/Family Advocate	$33,000
Special Assistance (attorney, therapist)	6,000
Supplement to other sources	
Child care and program services	4,000
Discretionary funds for families	4,000
Communication, general management	3,000
	$50,000

---

care program will have a variety of participants – leaders, attendees to most scheduled events, and families that receive services but do not participate in the group events. Even with active outreach, some families prefer to "go it alone" without letting anyone know the family situation.

In larger urban programs, a staff of coordinator, advocates who work one on one with families and other personnel will reach many more families with a much larger budget. Such programs may be the centralized guide for satellite Kinship Care groups in neighborhoods such as the *New York City Department for the Aging's Grandparent Resource Center* (212) 442-1094.

Basically, then, for under $50,000 a strong comprehensive program for kinship care can be developed in any small or mid-size community. Folks dedicated to establishing a well-rounded Comprehensive Kinship Care program can promote lots of support for the children in their community.

Funding Big and Small

So where does the money come from to support a strong Comprehensive Kinship Care program?

Every community is served by some government programs – our tax dollars at work, doing what they should do – stimulating the health of communities throughout the country. The best of these are Education, Social Services, and Infrastructure.

Social Service programs serve many areas: community health, mental health, and financial assistance to families in need. The programs under the various departments are always under some scrutiny. Assistance programs vary considerably from State to State though the names may seem the same such as the federally funded Temporary Assistance to Needy Families (TANF).

Under general funds like TANF, grants with names like "Strong Families, Safe Children" may be funneled to communities to establish diverse programs that will indeed increase the strength of the family. Community organizations such as Community Action Agencies, Senior Centers, Health Departments, Domestic Assault shelters apply to Social Services for a piece of the funds to implement a program that fits the criteria of the grant.

A well-defined Kinship Care Program requested by a social serving agency may be approved for funding by a local body charged with getting the funds to the right places, often the local Department of Health and Human Services. Part of the program design is to explain how the money will be spent and accountability procedures. This is generally the money to pay for a coordinator, special assistance services, and some incidentals as we have discussed.

These funds are carefully monitored and sometimes

require serving a particular population. Some programs funded by TANF, for instance, are required to serve a larger percent of folks matching the "needy family" criteria. To receive the funding means that all clients may have to sign an income statement and that the program has to work hard at maintaining the large percent of "needy families". These rules can frustrate good intentions. Many grandfamilies are not poor, not rich, but not really poor either. Many do not want to be associated with being "poor". Yet a specifically focused kinship care program can be extremely desirable to providers. The uniqueness of kinship care families is not equally addressed by government programs that try to support families.

The government sponsored programs are so valuable, but often government and national organization funding require some specifics that force applicants to rearrange their program. One program coordinator told me her kinship care program was funded by Zero to Three Funds through the social services department and so was restricted to families with children under three years old. Talk about frustration!

Some of the factors to consider when learning about and applying for funding:

1. A <u>combination funding plan</u> is critical – one or two major sources (government and foundation, for example), fundraising activities, and specific supplement sources.
2. All funding sources require accountability both in dollar numbers and numbers and types of population served. Have an accountant on board to keep track of these two areas.
3. Budgets must be clearly defined for all parties concerned (on *their* forms, be adaptable),
4. Grants take time, plan ahead. Deadlines for submissions are strict. Plan two or three weeks preparation. Expect months before notification. Be prepared for rejection.

The Grant Time Frame

| The Idea | Research/ Writing | Deadline | Wait |

Plan at least one to two months from idea to Deadline! Plan 6 to 10 weeks wait for an acceptance or rejection.

If the grant is due in February, count back to December to get the grant preparation done. Expect a response in April or May. If accepted, don't expect funds until June. Not all grants are on this time frame. Always read all instructions for RFP's (Request for Funding Programs) – grant applications.

5. Many starting programs supported by special start-up funds will last a few years in order to launch the project, but then funding dwindles or is withdrawn after a certain time. Sadly, many programs become dependent on the launching provider and neglect to develop a longer term funding plan to take over when the start-up service is complete.

6. Where the money goes in non-profits is always a concern to the public, as it should be. Developing a comprehensive vision of the program can help define the organization to the public. For instance, though 2/3rds of the dollar amount of the budget goes to pay

the Coordinator, *it is what the coordinator does with work time* that is the definition of the program:
- The Coordinator devotes 25% of time to community education,
- 60% of time to advocacy and serving the participants,
- 10% of the time to funding maintenance of the program (grant writing),
- and 5% administrative (filling out reports).

This gives a clearer picture of what the program is actually doing.

Where are the Funding Sources

If the organization has been taken under the wing of a larger non-profit, some of the funding will be covered by the larger organization . . . but not all. It is likely that the larger organization has applied to some other source appropriate to them such as Area Agency on Aging to help launch the program.

Other combination funding can be sought at places like the Brookdale Foundation, or a local urban foundation that prioritizes children and youth. Brookdale is a national foundation that specifically focuses on Kinship Care (thank goodness!) and is a good source for advice on establishing a program www.brookdalefoundation.org.

Other resources are noted in the last section of the book, **Resources, Resources, Resources**. A newly formed group with a funding leader would do well to learn from many sources what opportunities are available and how to access appropriate funding. Many states have organizations that offer grant writing workshops for non-profits.

Many community organizations are more than willing to offer smaller grants for specific projects – local service clubs, associations such as the local attorney association, or a medical group. This all comes back to the old adage, *Seek and you will find.* Just remember that what you are seeking matches your mission statement.

The Active Comprehensive Kinship Care Program

Now let's talk in depth about some of the supportive things a Comprehensive Kinship Care program can do.

Arrange Informational and Support Meetings

 Meetings should be at a predicable place, a predictable time and day of the month: such as "third Thursdays of the month, 7:30 p.m.". One meeting a month for information is about all most busy relatives can arrange.

Some programs also have a support group meeting with a therapist at a different time and more often – biweekly, weekly. Support groups with a therapist on hand are a special kind of gathering. As many of you know, the kinship family experiences an array of emotional and curious events raising their new family members. Children who have excessive fearful or aggressive responses in their daily lives often confound and confuse their caregivers. Every action/reaction seems to build on the previous action. Families need professional help and the help of their peers who are experiencing the same surprises. Therapy support groups are invaluable to the developing strength of relative care families. These sessions can greatly enhance the other critical elements of a comprehensive kinship care program.

The place for meetings should accommodate adults and children separately but near each other in comfortable settings. The place should also allow for snacks including coffee, tea, etc.

Refreshments bring people to gatherings – simple, easy to eat (and clean up) snacks are good, especially if they are healthful for adults and children. Sometimes local stores or bakeries want to donate to family-oriented organizations. Send thank you notes to the donating group with the amount they donated noted for their tax deductions. Staff and volunteers should plan to clean up afterwards, turn off and clean up the coffeemaker. There are numerous stories of the coffee pot anxieties after being left on all night in a locked building.

Some programs can actually have meals through a sponsoring agency such as a local Senior Services Center. Family meals together (free) are also a time of respite from all the other responsibilities kin families have taken on.

The Coordinator should make all arrangements in a timely manner beginning with advertisements for the monthly program in a regional newspaper. If the community is fortunate enough to have a local radio or TV station that covers community notices, these resources should be used extensively. Notices in the bulletins of faith organizations have deadlines and policies that should be checked and placed on a schedule of community announcements. The parent organization should also have resources available to make announcements of meetings.

30 Topic Ideas for Kinship Care Informational Meetings

Topic Idea	Suggested Source to Present
Household Safety	Community Health Dept or University Extension Office
How to Use a Computer	Local Computer experts or Regional Education Office
Internet Safety for children	Local police or Sheriff organization
Legalities	Legal aid, attorney in family issues, family court judge
Social Services	Social service personnel
Club drugs, street drugs	Health Dept. or Law enforcement Drug unit
Lead poisoning prevention	Health Department

Topic Idea	Suggested Source to Present
Understanding HIV/AIDS	Health Department
Saving for College	Investment or tax expert
Kinship Care tax deductions	Tax person
Social Security Benefits	Social Security Administration personnel
Community Jobs for Teens	Local Youth Job Service
Senior Health issues	Senior Service Center or Health Department
Nutritional meals, snacks	Health Department or University Extension Office
Health on tight budget	University Extension Office
Attention Deficit Disorder	Regional Education Resource
Grief and Loss	Therapist, Community Mental Health
Uncontrolled anger	Therapist, Community Mental Health
Keeping Fit	Personal Trainer, Physical Therapist
Teaching Children Money	University Extension Office
Life Saving Techniques	Red Cross or Specific health group
Living with Diabetes	Health Department, Hospital
Great holidays on a budget	University Extension Office
Getting to know each other	Therapist
Telling Stories	
Community Resources	United Way staff, Collaboration Director
School Issues	School counselor, Regional Education Resource
The TV Debate	
Getting Organized	Kinship Care Coordinator
Second Time Around	Kinship Care Coordinator

Quality, Safe Child Care
Many kinship care groups begin with someone's teenager "watching" the children for child care. Though this seems to be a money-saving means of addressing the issue of child care

during adult meetings, in a Comprehensive Kinship Care program, the Child Care piece must meet the standards of a Non-Profit organization in order to secure funding. That means paid educators offering an actual age-appropriate activity experience for the children. Some organized groups hire child therapists for this time to help children in group therapy settings.

Whether casual child activities under the guidance of professional educators or child therapy sessions, being with other children who are experiencing the relative care situation has as much healing opportunity for children as it does for adults. When quality child care exists, relatives feel good about their child's safety and the children feel good about coming to the meetings. The cost, ironically, is not much more than paying a babysitter. The baby sitter child care program helps valuable Kinship Care meetings to happen and we appreciate that effort. However, the Quality Child Care plan of a Comprehensive Kinship Care program has so much more to offer, including money funded because of the non-profit status.

The Quality Child Care <u>staff</u> for regular kinship care meetings should:

- Pass law enforcement background checks
- Possess a Bachelor or Masters degree in their professional field - early childhood or elementary education or child psychology
- Have 3-5 years education experience working with children and families
- Be trained in CPR and other emergency responses
- Come to the program with loving recommendations.

The Kinship Care program should:

- Prepare a written agreement defining what is expected of the Child Care Staff

- Including hourly or project pay and timeframe of pay (these are funding process issues required by many non-profit organizations in order to secure funding)
- Identify times of service and an expectation of type of programming
- Support the Child Care staff with refreshments and the supplies they might need.

One child care team in a Midwest kinship care program, could write a book of their own filled with all the unique activities they have developed for all ages of children. They have been certified as Early Childhood specialists with many years in local pre-school programs. Knowing that 4 to 13 year olds would also be in their group of 12 to 20 children, they set up activities that allowed older children to help younger children. They developed an array of hands-on activities to stories that the older children read to younger ones. They were not afraid to mix concoctions to the delight of the children such as the day they read Green Eggs and Ham and then made green eggs on Dr. Seuss' birthday. They grew little oak trees in milk cartons from the oak outside the Senior Center where the group met, then planted the trees at the Spring Kinship Care picnic. At the winter holidays, the team started out organizing talent shows that were later shared with kinship care parents.

The Child Care team shared a conversation between two ten-year-olds during the child care activity. One boy, Mike, was new to the program, the other, Aaron, had been in the program for a couple of years. While the boys were stirring up flour clay for the children's project, Mike asked Aaron why he was there. Aaron answered that when he was five his mom died and father couldn't raise him so he moved in with his grandmother. "What about you?" Aaron asked. Mike openly and without tears said, "My dad killed my mom then killed himself so my grandmother took my sister and me." Aaron looked at Mike, "That's tough," he said. In relating the story the child care staff added later, "As if they shared a bond in crisis, they nodded to each other then went on to help the four-year-olds make clay animals."

Special Assistance Services

Grandparents and other relatives often express on surveys that the two areas they need the most help with are finding Therapy and Legal issues. Some programs have Special Assistance funds that address these needs in the Kinship Care budget. These funds are drawn upon as needed, case by case. Some legal work may be offered pro bono – free under certain terms. Three to five thousand dollars budgeted for these areas allow kinship care providers and the Attorney or the Therapist to see families without fear of cutting into the family's already limited income.

The organization's funds for these issues may come from the basic budget and managed within their own category. A good example in one kinship care program: The program budgeted a few thousand dollars for attorney fees on the expectation that most of the counsel time used by families would be for consultation and some filing fees. An agreement was drawn up between the organization and the attorney, and the budget funds put into a trust in the account of a family law attorney (as noted in the agreement). Some budgeted funds were held for other attorneys in case a family had a conflict with the Kinship Care attorney under agreement. The comfort level of kinship care providers increased significantly when they were not burdened with the intimidating costs of hiring an attorney, or the difficulty in some cases of trying to live without legal consultation. Allocations from the local attorney association and other sources such as service clubs helped to build this item of the Kinship Care Program budget.

The private practice therapist, on the other hand, was already part of the program through contracts with Social Services. Arrangements for special funding through the social services department were extended or specifically developed to take on new families through the Kinship Care Program.

Negotiating these kinds of agreements requires someone who knows the local systems and has a community rapport to accomplish such support.

Discretionary Funds

Margaret, the Coordinator/Advocate for a Kinship Care program in one of the Atlantic Coast states was approached by Janice, grandmother of three children who were awarded a scholarship to the local YMCA camp. However, the children had no sleeping bags or other camp needs. Margaret smiled, handed Janice the gift card to the local all-purpose department store to buy the things she needed. "Try to keep it under $75 and bring the receipt when you bring the card back. "This is Our card," Margaret explained. "Our families share the card for needs such as the camp equipment."

Because kinship caregivers are proud and avoid the stigma that some perceive from helping programs, some kinship care programs have established *gift cards* from the discretionary funds to be used at large local retail department stores. The kinship caregiver can use the card to buy the needed school clothes, baby items or whatever is needed. The card is returned to the program with a copy of the receipt of items purchased and the balance noted for the next user. This type of discretionary fund use requires trust, of course, and honesty about the needs. However, programs that use this method have reported that the card has helped not only in trust building, but in the strong sense of community among the families. Some retail companies have even matched the funds available from the Kinship Care Program.

Discretionary funds are a valuable resource for any helping program because of the flexibility of use while supporting the families.

Advisory Board

When Kinship care programs become part of other organizations, there is the risk of bureaucracy and losing focus. The importance of establishing an Advisory Board of kinship care participants is to help the program to stay focused on the task of improving the lives of kinship care families, particularly grandparents raising grandchildren.

Meeting monthly at an hour convenient to the members of the Advisory Board, these folks listen to the coordinator's report of happenings in the program, and future projections. Their role should be to offer suggestions on activities, comment on issues facing the coordinator, and even to set policy in some situations.

An example of policy that one Kinship Care Advisory Board faced was how much support the program could offer kinship families that care for the children 2/3rds of the time daily, while the parent worked two or more jobs. In this case the program advisors decided that such families did not quite fit into the program of full time relative care and so, would not be eligible for some of the more costly parts of the program. However, the Advisory Board recognized a need for grandparent caregivers to be together to share their own unique issues and so encouraged the local senior center to offer a child care program and coffee klatch for the daytime grandparents. The outcome was a special caregivers program that offered respite, companionship of other caregivers in the same situation and some special informational speakers particularly on early childhood development.

Policy is strengthened when an Advisory Board agrees to wording and signs the policy as documentation to the parent organization that the policy is a legitimate concern addressed by the kinship care group. All policies should have a time limit on them and a process of revisiting to see if the policies work or are still relevant. Things change. Human Service programs should be adaptable to change as well.

Other Great Activities of Comprehensive Kinship Care Programs

The creativity of kinship care groups across the country is endless. Recognizing the needs of these very special families, the programs have become like families themselves filling the needs of individual members and providing a comfort home where information and camaraderie can thrive. These projects have included:

- Seasonal picnics
- Respite periods such as summer or holidays
- Grandparent pampering days
- College intern tutors
- Kinship care library with books, family oriented movies, magazines
- Conferences – regional, like expanded local meetings with information and   activities for wider group of children
- Computer library – including take home computers to learn on

- Online blogs or chat rooms helping each other through specific issues
- Shared cookbooks
- Warm lines (less urgent than Hotlines) where questions can be answered by a person who understands kinship care issues.

These are just a few ideas funded through special small grants, community gifts, or an array of donations.

This section of *A Kinship Guide* on how to develop a comprehensive Kinship Care Program is like a book within a book. I felt it was important to include the information because too many good intentions are lost on barriers that could be overcome. As long as there are kinship care families struggling through the criss-cross network of public systems, there should be an organization available to address each family's specific needs. If you don't already have access to the joys and support of other relatives raising their family's children, start with a simple outreach for a Meet Up. Before long your group will be able to establish a long lasting, high quality, Comprehensive Kinship Care Program. Do it for the children.

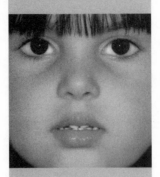

Resources, Resources, Resources.

Resources by Topic

State Departments of Health and Human Services

State Contacts for Central Kinship Care

Books on Kinship Care

States Census Chart

Resources by Topic

This is a difficult section to present to you because needs for resources are as specific as individual families, resources themselves often change, and there are so many places to find the information that may help in certain situations. I tried to categorize the following resources in a logical manner, but as anyone who has ever worked in an office knows when looking for information in a file, one person's "logic" is completely different from another. Please browse the entire list with commentaries; they may not be, in your mind, in the correct category.

Throughout this guidebook the emphasis has been on the importance of becoming an advocate for the children and yourselves in this new world of Kinship Care. Part of the advocacy is becoming a detective in finding the right resources for your need, questioning, cross referencing, listening to others, taking notes.

Think Locally

Many of the national organizations listed have a directory of local affiliates. Finding a local resource leads to others that eventually offer exactly the right connection for you. Being able to search online is the key to many successful searches. Even if you call a national organization you will likely be directed to check the online "site map" for a local affiliate. See the Finding Resources section on how to get "online".

Ben and Maria, retired, on Social Security and a small pension, began caring for their two young granddaughters in the middle of winter. Suddenly their extra costs cut severely into their very tight budget. They called their local Community Action Agency for help to avoid the threatened heat shut off. CAA staff received the couple and helped with their concern. Just as they were leaving Ben asked if they knew of anyone that could answer a legal question without charging a big retainer. When the CAA helper heard their kinship care story she opened a number of doors for them through the Kinship Care Center in the community, the Health Department and the legal aid advisor at the CAA office. "I'm so glad I asked," Ben told the worker.

Once again, ask questions if you don't find the help you need in the first place.

Learn the Tools

The chapters in this book on Getting Organized and Finding Resources are intended to strengthen the caregiver's ability to advocate by having the necessary paperwork and accessing the communication tools – telephone and computers. People are also good resources. If you need help to access a specific resource go to those places that have people who can help – the Senior Center, Community Action Agency, Library, Chamber of Commerce, United Way, Schools. When you go to one website for information, look around the site for other resources as well, called links (remember the rule about links – they can take you far away from your interest. Try to stay focused.)

There are a few national organizations that are the strength of research and reporting on behalf of kinship care families: AARP, Brookdale Foundation, CWLA, CDF, and Generations United. Look to these folks for back up information when you need to make a point.

National Organizations that have a Focus on Kinship Care or Grandparents as Parents

American Association for Retired Persons AARP,
Grandparent Information Center
601 E Street, NW
Washington DC 20049
1888-OUR-AARP (1-888-687-2277)
www.aarp.org or www.giclocalsupport.org or e-mail:
gic@aarp.org

AARP Grandparent Information Center offers a free newsletter on all grandparent issues, resources, state fact sheets that also list more local resources, and an e-mail address for personal contact.

Annie E. Casey Foundation
701 Sr. Paul St.
Baltimore, MD 21202
410-547-6600
www.aecf.org

The foundation is the strongest support for research through the Kids Count data. In addition the Annie E. Casey Foundation sponsors programs that strengthen all children and families.

The Brookdale Foundation Group
950 Third Avenue, 19th Floor
New York, NY 10022
www.brookdalefoundation.org

Brookdale has been a crowning force in providing seed money to establish local programs for relatives and grandparents in kinship care. Most of the RAPP, Relatives As Parents, Programs began with the help of the Brookdale Foundation. Requests for Funding Programs are offered every year with lots of help to get established. Check online for more information.

Children's Defense Fund, CDF
25 E Street NW
Washington, DC 20001
202-628-8787 or 800-CDF-1200 (800-233-1200)
www.childrensdefense.org

Children's Defense Fund is a strong supportive lobby for children's issues in the nation's capitol. Some publications on general children's issues are available.

Child Welfare League of America, CWLA
2345 Crystal Drive, Suite 250
Arlington, VA 22202
703-412-2400
www.cwla.org

Child Welfare League of America with members from child welfare areas nationwide sponsors and reports on significant research regarding the welfare of children including foster care and kinship care. CWLA joins with other national child lobby groups to ensure that legislators know the issues involving America's children. CWLA offers a number of publications particularly reports of research and the impact on the society. In addition, those of us who work with kinship care issues can receive online news alerts that include funding sources, conferences, and other critical information.

Community Action Agencies
Community Action Partnership
1140 Connecticut Ave., Suite 1210
Washington, DC 20036
202-265-7546
www.communityactionpartnership.com
e-mail: info@communityactionpartnership.com

The website and national offices provide a link to 1000 Community Action Agencies around the country all helping to lift individuals out of poverty and strengthen the health of communities. Many services are provided under the umbrella of these agencies including the management of Head Start and other pre-school programs in some local agencies.

Grandsplaces
154 Cottage Road
Enfield, CT 06082
www.grandsplace.org
Kathy@grandsplace.org

The website is very good with lots of connections to state sources. There may be an update problem with the site owners. It is very difficult to maintain such vast information as a private individual. Keep trying with this one.

Generations United
1331 H Street NW, Suite 900
Washington, DC 20005
202-289-3979
www.gu.org
e-mail: gu@gu.org

Another member of the hard-working coalition of organizations working to improve the conditions for kinship care families, Generations United maintains an excellent website that reports on research including states guardianship subsidies.

Kinship Information Network, Inc
PO box 450063
Sunrise, FL 33345-0063
772-501-0502
www.kinsupport.org

An interesting website for Grandparents and other Relatives written by families going through the many issues involved in kinship care.

National Indian Child Welfare Association NICWA
5100 S.W. Macadam Avenue, Suite 300
Portland, Oregon 97239
503-222-4044
www.nicwa.org

Serving over 500 tribes in the country, NICWA offers many services on behalf of Indian Child Welfare including assistance with kinship care inquiries. For specific family issues involving an Indian child begin your inquiry with the local Department of Health and Human Services.

National Indian Council on Aging, Inc
10501 Montgomery Blvd. N.E., Suite 210
Albuquerque, NM 87111
505-292-2001
www.nicoa.org
e-mail: info@nicoa.org

Serving the nation's American Indian and Alaska Native elders with information and referral on all issues concerning aging including kinship care.

National Committee of Grandparents for Children's Rights
School of Social Welfare HSC, 1.2., Rm 093
Stony Brook University
Stony Brook, NY 11794-8231
1-866-624-9900
www.grandparentsforchildren.org

Kinship issues are a part of the larger grandparent experience for this organization. The website also offers information from legal research and a helpline.

Social Security Administration
Windsor Park Building
6401 Security Blvd.
Baltimore, MD 21235
1-800-772-1213, TTY # 1-800-325-0778
www.ssa.gov
Also www.insurekidsnow.gov

1-877-KIDS-NOW (1-877-543-7669) for The Children's Health Insurance Program direction to individual state programs. Also known as SCHIP – States Children's Health Insurance Program.

The Social Security Administration is a very valuable resource to millions of Americans. SSA also helps with kinship care questions.

Disability claims are in difficulty at this writing, so expect a waiting time. However the questions of benefits for children or spouses can be answered quickly. Filing for lost cards, name change, or other small concerns usually can be processed quickly as well. Explore the online site, particularly the frequently asked questions.

Federal Citizen Information Center
Dept. WWW
Pueblo, CO 81009
www.usa.gov
1.800.333.4636 or 800 FED INFO

The source for U.S. Government publications and forms for information on business, non-profits, citizen concerns. Also check out www.pueblo.gsa.gov Federal Citizen Information Center (1.888.878.3256 or 1.888.8PUEBLO).

Child Resources

About Our Kids
577 First Avenue
New York, NY 10016
(212) 263-6622
www.aboutourkids.org

A project of New York University Child Study Center and the University School of Medicine, this valuable website offers information on a multitude of child subjects.

Adoption.Com
1745 S. Alma School Road, Suite 215
Mesa, Arizona 85210
480-446-0500, 9-5 Mountain time
www.adoption.com

A very sophisticated website that will key in to the state you are writing from before you even ask. Study the website for information relating to kinship adoptions. Lots of information.

Big Brothers Big Sisters National Office
230 North 13th Street
Philadelphia, PA 19107
215-567-7000
www.bbbsa.org

There is so much data to support this mentoring program. Explore the website for information. Also check on local mentoring programs in your community including Boys and Girls Clubs.

Center for Children of Incarcerated Parents
PO Box 41-286
Eagle Rock, California 90041
626-449-2470
www.e-ccip.org
e-mail: ccip@earthlink.net

Focusing on articles and training this is the only site I could find on this important subject. Be sure to check locally for programs that assist family and especially children of incarcerated parents.

Child Abuse: Childhelp's National Child Abuse Hotline
800-4-A-CHILD (800-422-4453)

Child Welfare Information Gateway
Children's Bureau/ACYF
1250 Maryland Avenue, SW
Eighth Floor
Washington, DC 20024
703-385-7565 or 800-394-3366
www.childwelfare.gov

An excellent resource for answering all sorts of kinship care questions especially about adoption or guardianship. Includes valuable links.

Grief: Compassionate Friends, Inc.
PO Box 3696
Oak Brook, IL 60522-3696
877-969-0010 (toll free)
630-990-0010
www.compassionatefriends.org

A source for families experiencing grief due to death, with a separate help for children who have lost parents.

Child Care: National Association of Child Care Resources and Referral Agencies NCCRRA
3101 Wilson Blvd., Suite 350
Arlington, VA 22201
703-341-4100
www.naccrra.org
Also: **Child Care Aware** www.childcareaware.org
1-800-424-2246

These two organizations are closely associated by providing valuable links to local child care resources. They also produce excellent material on child care training and site help.

Early On
13109 Schavey Road, Suite 4
DeWitt, Michigan 498820
www.1800earlyon.org
1-800-EARLYON or 1-800-327-5966

Early On is borne of federal legislation – Part C of the Individuals with Disabilities Education Act – however, Michigan seems to be the leading program in the country in my research. Check locally with Intermediate School Districts or to learn more about the exceptional Michigan program contact EarlyOn Michigan for some help.

National Head Start Association
1615 Prince St.
Alexandria, VA 22314
703-739-0875
www.nhsa.org

Serving one million children, this superior program is exemplified in its excellent website. This is a private non-profit organization funded in a great part by federal dollars. Study the website to find a local program.

YMCA of the USA
101 North Wacker Drive
Chicago, IL 60606
800-872-9622
www.ymca.net

An excellent resource in communities with programs for all ages. Some more comprehensive Y's have the ability to sponsor an organization such as a Kinship Care Support Group. The website provides a directory to local YMCA facilities.

Zero to Three
National Center for Infants, Toddlers and Families
2000M St. NW Suite 200
Washington, DC 20036
www.zerotothree.org

Zero to Three is a research and reporting organization on the healthy development of infants and toddlers. Their list of publications and regular newsletter are valuable to any organization or family working with early childhood development.

Health Issues

Alcohol and Substance Abuse

A.A. World Services, Inc.
PO Box 459
New York, NY 10163
212-870-3400
www.alcoholics-anonymous.org

Al-Anon Family Group Headquarters, Inc.
1600 Corporate Landing Parkway
Virginia Beach, VA 23454
757-563-1600
www.al-anon.alateen.org

American Social Health Association Sexually Transmitted Diseases
PO Box 13827
Research Triangle Park, NC 27709
919-361-8400
www.ashastd.org
STI Resource Center Hotline 1-800-227-8922

Cocaine Anonymous CAWSO
3740 Overland Ave. Suite C
Los Angeles, CA 90034 or
    CAWSO
    PO Box 492000
    Los Angeles, CA 90049-8000
    International Referral Line 1-800-347-8998
    www.ca.org

Cocaine Anonymous supports users who want to quit with information on local meetings, publications and other resources.

Children of Alcoholics Foundation
164 West 74th Street
New York, NY 10023
646-505-2060
www.coaf.org

Serving with information and referral, the foundation is one of many resources working to prevent this anxious disease from continuing in families.

Learning Disabilities

CHADD
 National Office of children and adults with Attention deficit/hyperactivity disorder
8181 Professional Place, Suite 150
Landover, MD 20785
301-306-7070
800-233-4050
www.chadd.org

Another valuable information and referral group. A very informative updated website.

Learning Disabilities Association of America
4156 Library Road
Pittsburgh, PA 15234-1349
412-341-1515
www.ldaamerica.org

Another very informative website covering a wide range of learning disabilities. Help for families as well as professionals.

National Dissemination Center for children with Disabilities
PO Box 1492
Washington, DC 20013
800-695-0285
www.nichcy.org
e-mail: nichcy@aed.org

Offering information on a number of disabilities affecting children.

<u>**Physical and Mental Health**</u>

Centers for Disease Control CDC
National Prevention Information Network
PO Box 6003
Rockville, MD 20849-6003
1-800-458-5231
International 1-404-679-3860
www.cdc.gov

Use the Search Box on the website to type in the key words of your concern. Issues on every conceivable medical issue is covered including Fetal Alcohol Syndrome and other infant issues.

Hospice Foundation of America
www.hospicefoundation.org
1-800-854-3402

A thorough website with lots of information including assistance to local programs.

Hospice Net
Suite 51
401 Bowling Avenue
Nashville, TN 37205-5124
www.hospicenet.org children and Death

About Our Kids
New York University Child Study Center
577 First Ave.
New York, NY 10016
212-263-6622
www.aboutourkids.org

National Kidney Foundation, Inc.
30 East 33rd Street
New York, NY 10016
1-800-622-9010
www.kidney.org

National Institutes of Health NIH
9000 Rockville Pike
Bethesda, Maryland 20892
301-496-4000
www.nih.gov

Once you get on to the National Institutes of Health website you will recognize why it is plural – institutes. This valued federal organization has an institute in various major areas covering the health of Americans. Following are some of those specifically noted. If you go to the NIH website you can also reach any of the other sites.

Also of interest **National Institute of Health Senior Health** covering Alzheimer's Arthritis, Depression and many other senior health issues: www.nihseniorhealth.gov.

National Institute of Child Health and Human Development
PO Box 3006
Rockville, MD 20847
1-800-370-2943 TTY 1-888-320-6942
www.nichd.nih.gov

National Institute of Mental Health
Science Writing, Press, and Dissemination Branch
6001 Executive Boulevard, Room 8184, MSC 9663
Bethesda, MD 20892-9663
301-443-4513 (local)
1-866-615-6464 (toll-free)
301-443-8431 (TTY)
1-866-415-8051 (TTY toll-free)
www.nimh.nih.gov

National Coalition Against Domestic Violence NCADV
1120 Lincoln Street, Suite 1603
Denver, CO 80203
303-839-1852 TTY 303-839-1681
www.ncadv.org

Working to end violence in the lives of individuals, this coalition of organizations offers information and referral.

Legal

American Bar Association
321 N. Clark St.
Chicago, IL 60610
1-800-285-2221
www.abanet.org

This is an excellent central source for information or finding an attorney locally as well as research and news on all things legal.

Chance at Childhood
238 Baker Hall
Michigan State University
East Lansing, MI 48824
517-432-8406 1-866-725-8406
chanceatchildhood.msu.edu

The Chance at Childhood Law and Social work Clinic offers legal representation to children as well as consultation to the families and professionals involved in cases. At the same time, the Law students and Graduate students in social work gain critical experience in both fields while earning dual certification. The Chance at Childhood Clinic is a unique service training program.

National Association for Community Mediation
1514 Upshur Street NW
Washington, DC 20011
Phone: (202) 545-8866
www.nafcm.org

The website offers a search to find local mediation resources.

Careers and Financial Aid

Finaid
www.finaid.org

Finaid is a comprehensive website resource on all aspects of financial aid for advanced education including an extensive data base. This is a Monster.Com affiliate.

Union Plus Scholarship Data Base
American Education Services (ACS)
1200 N. 7th St.
Harrisburg, PA 17102
1-877-881-1022
http://unionplus.educationplanner.com

This site offers a data base of scholarships and other benefits to members of several unions nationwide.

College Savings Plan Network

To find a 529 plan locator in your state check the **College Savings Plan Network** at www.collegesavings.org an affiliate of National Association of State Treasurers.

Scholarships from Fortune 500:
www.collegescholarships.org/Fortune500.htm

Internet Safety Resources

www.wiredsafety.org

A comprehensive website with sections for caregivers and sections for children. Lots of room to ask specific questions.

www.isafe.org

A focus on student use of computers at school. Also includes parental help and information specifically for children.

www.esrb.org

Entertainment rating system for video games. Lots of news and updates on games as well.

www.netlingo.com

A popular site for all text users. This site also offers awareness of text lingo for parents.

State Departments of Health and Human Services

As we have stated throughout this project, states have many names for their federally and state funded Department of Health and Human Services. This valuable service in our country is a tremendous resource for kinship care providers, just as kinship care providers are a tremendous resource for the States' child welfare services – a department within the DHHS. Following are the names, websites and telephone numbers for the state office of each DHHS.

The S in parenthesis means the state is currently or has participated in some type of Guardianship Assistance support for relative caregivers. This data is as current as possible, however, as we keep saying, things change. Michigan for instance may have a Guardianship Assistance Subsidy before this book is actually on the market. We hope so.

Main Department Name, Website, Phone Number and Guardianship Subsidy status

Alabama Department of Human Resources (S)
http://www.dhr.state.al.us/list.asp
Phone Number: (334) 242-1310

Alaska Office of Children's Services (-)
http://www.hss.state.ak.us/ocs/
Phone: (907) 465-3170

Arizona Department of Economic Security (S)
http://www.azdes.gov/ASPNew/default.asp
Phone: (800) 308-9000

Arkansas Department of Human Services (-)
http://www.arkansas.gov/dhs/homepage.html
Phone: 1-800-235-0002

California Department of Social Services (S)
http://www.dss.cahwnet.gov/cdssweb FindServic_2312.
htm#top
Phone: (916) 651-8848

Colorado Department of Human Services (-)
http://www.cdhs.state.co.us/servicebyneed.htm
Phone: (303) 866-5700

Connecticut Department of Children and Families (S)
http://www.ct.gov/dcf/site/default.asp
Phone: (860) 550-6300

Delaware Department of Services for Children, Youth, and Their Families (S)
http://kids.delaware.gov/
Phone: (302) 633-2500

Florida Department of Children and Families (S)
http://www.myflorida.com/cf_web/
Phone: (850) 487-1111

Georgia Department of Human Resources - Division of Family and Children Services (S)
http://dfcs.dhr.georgia.gov/portal/site/DHR-DFCS/
Phone: (404) 651-9361

Hawaii Department of Human Services (S)
http://www.state.hi.us/dhs/
Phone: (808) 453-6357

Idaho Department of Health and Welfare (S)
http://www.healthandwelfare.idaho.gov/Default.aspx
Phone: (800) 926-2588

Illinois Department of Children and Family Services (S)
http://www.state.il.us/dcfs/index.shtml
Phone: (800) 232-3798

Indiana Family and Social Services Administration (-)
http://www.in.gov/fssa/
Phone: (317) 233-4454

Iowa Department of Human Services (-)
http://www.dhs.state.ia.us/index.html
Phone: (515) 281-5454

Kansas Department of Social and Rehabilitation Services (S)
http://www.srskansas.org/
Phone: (785) 296-3959

Kentucky Cabinet for Health and Family Services (S)
http://chfs.ky.gov/dcbs/
Phone: (800) 372-2973

Louisiana Department of Social Services (S)
http://www.dss.state.la.us/
Phone: (225) 342-0286

Maine Department of Health and Human Services (-)
http://www.maine.gov/dhhs/
Phone: (207) 287-3707

Maryland Department of Human Resources (S)
http://www.dhr.state.md.us/
Phone: (800) 332-6347

Massachusetts Department of Social Services (S)
http://www.mass.gov/dss/
Phone: (617) 748-2000

Michigan Department of Human Services (-)
http://www.michigan.gov/dhs
Phone: (517) 373-2035

Minesota Department of Human Services (S)
http://www.dhs.state.mn.us/
Phone: (651) 431-2000

Mississippi Department of Human Services (-)
http://www.mdhs.state.ms.us/
Phone: (800) 345-6347

Missouri Department of Social Services (S)
http://www.dss.mo.gov/
Phone: (573) 751-4815

Montana Department of Public Health and Human Services (S)
http://www.dphhs.mt.gov/
Phone: (406) 444-9500

Nebraska Department of Health and Human Services (S)
http://www.hhs.state.ne.us/
Phone: (402) 471-3121

Nevada Department of Health and Human Services - Division of Child and Family Services (S)
http://www.dcfs.state.nv.us/
Phone: (775) 684-4400

New Hampshire Department of Health and Human Services (-)
http://www.dhhs.state.nh.us/DHHS/DHHS_SITE/default.htm
Phone: (800) 852-3345

New Jersey Department of Human Services (S)
http://www.state.nj.us/humanservices/index.shtml
Phone: (609) 588-2400

New Mexico Children, Youth & Families Department (S)
http://www.cyfd.org/
Phone: (505) 827-7602

New York State Office of Children and Family Services (-)
http://www.ocfs.state.ny.us/main/
Phone: (518) 473-7793

North Carolina Division of Social Services (-)
http://www.dhhs.state.nc.us/dss/
Phone: (919) 733-3055

North Dakota Department of Human Services (S)
http://www.nd.gov/dhs/
Phone: (800) 472-2622

Ohio Department of Job and Family Services (-)
http://jfs.ohio.gov/
Phone: (614) 466-1213

Oklahoma Department of Human Services (S)
http://www.okdhs.org/
Phone: (405) 521-3646

Oregon Department of Human Services (S)
http://www.oregon.gov/DHS/
Phone: (503) 945-5944

Pennsylvania Department of Public Welfare (S)
http://www.dpw.state.pa.us/
Phone: (877) 4-PA-KIDS or (877) 472-5437

Rhode Island Department of Children, Youth & Families (S)
http://www.dcyf.state.ri.us/
Phone: (401) 528-3502

South Carolina Department of Social Services (-)
http://www.state.sc.us/dss/
Phone: (803) 898-7601

Tennessee Department of Children's Services (S)
http://www.state.tn.us/youth/
Phone: (615) 741-9701

Texas Department of Family and Protective Services (-)
http://www.dfps.state.tx.us/
Phone: (512) 438-4800

Utah Department of Human Services (S)
http://www.dhs.utah.gov/
Phone: (800) 662-3722

Vermont Family Services Division (-)
http://www.dcf.state.vt.us/fsd/
Phone: (802) 241-2131

Virginia Department of Social Services (-)
http://www.dss.virginia.gov/
Phone: (800) 552-3431

Washington Department of Social and Health Services (-)
http://www1.dshs.wa.gov/
Phone: (800) 760-5340

West Virginia Department of Health and Human Resources (S)
http://www.wvdhhr.org/
Phone: (304) 558-0684

Wisconsin Department of Health and Family Services (-)
http://dhfs.wisconsin.gov/
Phone: (608) 266-1865

Wyoming Department of Family Services (S)
http://dfsweb.state.wy.us/
Phone: (307)777-7564

District of Columbia Child and Family Services Agency (S)
http://www.cfsa.dc.gov/cfsa/site/default.asp
Phone: (202) 442-6000

State Contacts for Central Kinship Care

As we discussed previously Kinship Care resources are sparsely available on a nationwide basis. Following is a list of states that identified some kinship activity. The contact names and numbers change often. Some states are actively serving kinship care families. A note may be listed after these states along with some special activity (a booklet or website) or multiple sources of information from those states. Some programs are managed by the state Department of Health and Human Services others by a university extension or aging service organization.

Be sure to check regularly with the national AARP website (www.AARP.org). AARP tries hard to keep the information updated. We did the best we could on this list.

Alabama

Alabama Department of Senior Services, Letha Stuckey:
334-242-5743 or 1-877-425-2243
letha.stuckey@adss.alabama.gov,
http://www.AlabamaAgeline.gov
Find Local Coordinator: 1-800-243-5463

Alaska

Grandfamilies Network Project - Volunteers of America,
Tami Eller or Christina Lowther 888-522-9866 or
907-522-9866 (Anchorage)
grands@voaak.org, www.voaak.org

Arizona

Central Arizona Kinship Care Coalition, Beatitudes
Center for Developing Older Adult Resources (D.O.A.R.),
602-274-5022, www.centerdoar.org

Arkansas

Arkansas AARP, Susan Keuhner, Associate State Director,
501-217-1625, skuehner@aarp.org, www.aarp.org/ar

California

California has nearly one million children in kinship care,
the largest number of all 50 states. In response many
regional kinship care groups are addressing the needs of
families. Check the AARP Grandparent information, state
facts, to find a regional program. This listing may have more
information statewide: California Community Colleges,
State Chancellor's Office of the California Community
Colleges, Lucy Berger, Coordinator of Foster and Kinship
Care Education (FKCE), 916-323-5276, Lberger@cccco.edu,
64 participating community colleges throughout the state.

Colorado

Families First, Sarah Hite, Coordinator, 877-695-7996 (toll-
free in Colorado) 303-695-7996,
www.familiesfirstcolorado.org
info@familiesfirstcolorado.org; also Department Human
Services has booklet done in 2000 Kinship Care Resource
Guide – Grandparent Resource Center, Shirley Berens,
Director, 303-980-5707, e-mail: GRC4USA@aol.com

Connecticut
> Connecticut Department of Social Services, Aging Services Division – Grandparents As Parents (GAPS) Network, Roberta Gould, Caregiver Support Coordinator, at 860-424-5199 roberta.gould@ct.gov

Delaware
> GrandParents United DE, www.grandparentsunitedde.com, or www.grandparentunitedde.org. Delaware Health & Social Services Division of Services for Aging and Adults with Physical Disabilities, Carol Boyer, Joining Generations, at (302) 255-9390 or 1-800-223-9074 or carol.boyer@state.de.us, www.dhss.delaware.gov/dsaapd

District of Columbia
> Because such a large number of kinship families in the D.C. area are ethnically African-American, many of the excellent resources are designed to preserve the family. Be sure to also check the AARP website state fact sheet for more. Healthy Families/Thriving Communities Collaboratives, www.dccollaboratives.org covers 7 neighborhoods. Washington DC Child & Family Services Agency Grandparent Caregiver Pilot, Valorie Gainer, 202-442-6009, valorie.gainer@dc.gov

Florida
> Florida Kinship Center (University of South Florida) a premiere statewide service includes map of kinship programs, www.flkin.usf.edu, kinfo@flkin.org, 800.640.6444

Georgia
> Georgia Department of Human Resources, Division of Aging Services, Leslie Sessley, Kinship Care Coordinator, 404-657-8787, lesessley@dhr.state.ga.us www.hdr.georgia.gov/grg

Hawaii
> State of Hawaii Executive Office on Aging and Hawaii Caregiver coalition RAPP, Wes Lum wlwum@mail.health.state.hi.us, 808.586.7319, "Na Tutu – grandmothers"

Idaho

Idaho Kincare Coalition, www.idahoaging.com, Tina Rice trice@aging.idaho.gov, 208.334.3833.AARP, Cathy McDougal, cmcdougall@aarp.org, 208-855-4003. Idaho Cooperative Extension, Harriet Shaklee, 208-364-4016, hshaklee@uidaho.edu

Illinois

Grandparents and Other Relatives Raising Grandchildren, Project of Illinois, State Department on Aging, 800.252.8966, newsletter, Barb Schwartz, 217.524.5327, barb.schwartz@illinois.gov

Indiana

Indiana Family and Social Services Administration and Perdue Extension, Kate Tewanger at (317) 232-7148 or kathryn.tewanger@fssa.in.gov

Iowa

Iowa Department of Elder Affairs (DEA) Nicki Stajcar, 515.242.3320, nicki.stajcar@iowa.gov

Kansas

Kansas Children's Service League (KCSL) B.J. Gore, 316.942.4261 bjgore@kcsl.org, www.kcsl.org

Kentucky

Kentucky Division of Aging Services Marni Mountjoy at (502) 564-6930 (ext. 3385) or marni.mountjoy@ky.gov

Louisiana

Grandparents Raising Grandchildren Information Center of Louisiana – has newsletter, Dot Thibodeaux, 225.355.5442, lagrparinfo@yahoo.com or Danna Spayde.

Maine

University of Maine Center on Aging and School of social Work with Family Connections, RAPP Task Force – Parenting relatives, Dr. Lenard W. Kaye at the University of Maine Center on Aging at 207-581-3444 or len.kaye@umit.maine.edu

Maryland
Kinship Resource Center of Maryland, Central data Bank, Dr. Earlene Merrill, 888-951-4177, 410-951-4177, emerrill@coppin.edu, Maryland Kinship Care Program newsletter, www.dhr.state.md.us/ssa/kinship/ini.htm

Massachusetts
Check the AARP State Facts site for a local kinship care group, www.aarp.org > grandparenting > State Fact Sheets. Boston – Raising Our children's Children (ROCC) Harriet Jackson-Lyons, 617-541-3561. Legal help from Volunteer Lawyers Project, Lyn Girton, 617-423-0648, lgirton@vlnet.org

Michigan
Kinship Care Resource Center – Ama Agyemang, 517-355-9600, 800-535-1218, kinship@msu.edu statewide newsletter, contact list, conferences.

Minnesota
Minnesota Kinship Caregivers Association (MKCA) offers legal resource manual, includes six Regional Service Agencies that work directly with families. www.mkca.org, Sharon Durken 651.917.4642, sharon@mkca.org

Mississippi
Individual counties, no central. Dr. Sylvia Forster – Pinebelt Association for Families, 601.582.0909 brightpaff@aol.com

Missouri
University Extension Service Elizabeth Reinsch 314.615.2911, reinsche@missouri.edu, website: http://extension.missouri.edu/parentlink. Also offers a warm line for help: 1-800-552-8522

Montana
Montana State University Extension Service, Montana Grandparents Raising Grandchildren Project, Sandra Bailey 406.994.6745, baileys@montana.edu

Nebraska
RAPP, Marilyn Bauer at 402-470-0098 or mbauer@u-s-foods.com

Nevada
Nevada Parents Encouraging Parents and the Caring
Community Project, TJ Rosenberg, Collaboration
Coordinator, 702-388-8899, tjrosenberg@nvpep.org,
www.nvpep.org

New Hampshire
University of New Hampshire Cooperative Extension,
Thomas Linehan, 603-225-5505, 800-852-3345
www.nhrapp.org or charlene.baxter@unh.edu
www.extension.unh.edu

New Jersey
New Jersey Kinship Navigator Program 877.816.3211, Susan
Chermak, 609-588-2171, susan.chermak@dhs.state.nj.us
website: www.state.nj.us/humanservices/dfd/index.html

New Mexico
New Mexico Guardianship Project of Advocacy, Inc. Niki
Tantalou Collard, 1-866-376-9625 niki@nmadvocacy.org,
www.nmadvocacy.org; NICOA Indian Council on Aging,
alvin.rafelito@nicoa.org

New York
New York State Kinship Navigator Program can provide
info and referral statewide: www.nysnavigator.org toll-
free: 877-4KinInfo, 877-454-6463. New York State Office of
Children and Family Services (OCFS)
robert.resnick@dfa.state.ny.us or Frank Tamburro, Program
Manager for NYS sites.

North Carolina
North Carolina Division of Aging & Adult services, RAPP
Jody Riddle, 919.733.3983, jody.riddle@ncmail.net; North
Carolina Cooperative Extension, 919-515-9146, Dr. Luci
Bearon, luci_bearon@ncsu.edu

North Dakota
ND Aging and Disability Resource-LINK, 1-800-451-8693, www.carechoice.nd.gov e-mail carechoice@nd.gov
North Dakota Department of Human Services Aging Services Division, Judy Tschider, program administrator, 701-328-4643 or 1-800-451-8693 jtschider@nd.gov

Ohio
Ohio department of Jobs & Family Kinship Navigator 866.886.3537, Kristen Burgess, Ohio Department of Job and Family Services, 614-752-1329, burgek01@odjfs.state.oh.us

Oklahoma
Department of Human Services, Aging Services Division, Oklahoma Area-wide Service Information System (OASIS), 1-800-42-OASIS. LaNell Daniel 405-522-3073 or lanell.daniel@okdhs.org, http://www.okdhs.org/programsandservices/aging/grand/

Oregon
Oregon State University Extension Family & Development Program RAPP, Sally Bowman, bowmans@oregonstate.edu 541-737-1020

Pennsylvania
Department on Aging & Extension Penn State, at www.aging.state.pa.us. Bob McNamara at 717-783-6207 or rmcnamara@state.pa.us

Rhode Island
Rhode Island Department on Elderly Affairs, Maria Nunez, 401.462.0507, maria@dea.state.ri.us

South Carolina
The Lieutenant Governor's Office on Aging, Area Agencies on Aging, Councils on Aging and local community service providers, Eve Barth, 803.734.9872, barthe@aging.sc.gov, www.aging.sc.gov

South Dakota
Grandparents as Parents support, Sharon Hall, 605.361.2645, slh@sio.midco.net

Tennessee

Department of Children's Service (DCS) Relative Caregiver
Support, Robert Matthews, Director, Resource Linkage,
Department of Children's Services at 615-253-2342 or
robert.L.matthews@state.tn.us

Texas

The Texas Department of Aging & Disability Services,
Access & Assistance - Area Agencies on Aging DADS AAA
hotline at 800-252-9240, Betty Ford, Director, Area Agencies
on Aging Section, at 512-438-4120 or
betty.ford@dads.state.tx.us,
http://www.dads.state.tx.us/contact/combined.cfm

Utah

Utah Department of Human Services, Division of Family
Services RAPP, Judy Hull, 801.538.4372,
judymiller@utah.gov

Vermont

Vermont Kin as Parents (VKAP) Lynn Granger,
Coordinator, 802-338-4725 or kinlmg@comcast.net website:
www.vermontkinasparents.org

Virginia

Department for Aging Kinship Care Initiative Task Force &
Information (VDA) Ellen Nau, 804) 662-9340,
ellen.nau@vda.virginia.gov

Washington

http://parenting.wsu.edu/relative/index.htm
Cooperative Extension Navigator RAPP, Washington's
Kinship Caregivers Support Program (KCSP) is for
kinship caregivers who are not involved with the formal
child welfare system Aging and Disability Services
Administration at 800-422-3263 or go to
http://www1.dshs.wa.gov/kinshipcare

West Virginia

RAPP West Virginia University Extension Allison Nichols, 304-293-2796 (ext. 3451), ahnichols@mail.wvu.edu website: www.wvrapp.org; Ashley Daniels, Mission West Virginia, at 304-562-0723, adaniels@missionwv.org; Laura Lou Harbert, Department of Health and Human Resources, 304-558-4303 or lauraharbert@wvdhhr.org

Wisconsin

Grandparents Raising Grandchildren Partnership of Wisconsin has a number of contacts that all work together: for questions outside Milwaukee - Holly Telfer, telfeHR@dhfs.state.wi.us; Milwaukee County questions to Mary Kennedy, kenneml@dhfs.state.wi.us; Barbara Robinson, Bureau of Aging & Disability Resources, 608-266-7498 or robinbj@dhfs.state.wi.us; website: http://www.uwex.edu/ces/flp/grandparent/relationships/

Wyoming

The Wyoming Department of Family Services, Zaffer Sharif, Social Services Consultant, 307-777-6203, zshari@state.wy.us. Dana Ward, dward@state.wy.us; Alice Carter, Wyoming Kinship Advocacy, alice@calc.net. The Wyoming Department of Health, Aging Division Kim Latta, Program Manager, National Family Caregiver Support Program, Wyoming Department of Health, Aging Division, 800-442-2766 or kimberly.latta@health.wyo.gov

Books on Kinship Care

To Grandma's House, We...Stay : When You Have to Stop
Spoiling Your Grandchildren and Start Raising Them by Sally
Houtman - Studio 4 Productions Publishing Co., 1999 & 2003
ISBN: 1882349059.
Very good for help on the home front. Author is a kin-raised
child now psychologist offering lots of support.

The Grandparent Guide - Arthur Kornhaber, 2002, McGraw Hill
ISBN: 0071383115
Though filled with general grandparent support, this guide
offers one good chapter on raising grandchildren.

Second Time Around: Help for Grandparents Who Raise Their
Children's Kids - Joan Callander Bookpartners, 1999
ISBN: 1581510217
This is a personal account of the experience of raising a
related child.

Raising Our Children's Children by Deborah Doucette-Dudman
Fairview Press, 1997
ISBN:1577490266
Psychological guidance through case studies.

Relatives Raising Children: An Overview of Kinship Care by
Joseph Crumbley - Children's Welfare League of America Press,
1997
ISBN: 0878686843
This is a practical guide from an excellent organization,
however currently out of print. The text has an emphasis on
foster grandparenting.

*Grandparents as Parents: A Survival Guide for Raising a Second
Family* by Sylvie De Toledo - Guilford Press, 1995
ISBN: 1572300205
Psychological support with practical guides. This was the
only book available for many years now more than a dozen
years old.

Kinship Care – Making the most of a Valuable Resource Edited
by Rob Geen - Urban Institute Press, Washington D.C., 2003
ISBN:087766718-7
This is a critical gathering of information for policy makers,
researchers, educators on Kinship Care issues.

Some inspirational books:

Robert Lives With His Grandparents by Martha Whitmore
Hickman - Albert Whitman & Co., 1995
ISBN: 0807570842
A children's book.

Tickleberry Hill Hilda Osborne - Authorhouse, 2003
ISBN: 1403390770
A personal account of the experience.

Pilgrim Prayers for Grandmothers Raising Grandchildren by
Giraurd Chase - Hollies Pilgrim Press, 2002
ISBN: 0829814906

States Census Chart

State	Children in Kinship Care	% of states children	Grandparent Caregivers
Alabama	113,122	10.0%	51,486
Alaska	10,808	5.7%	5,110
Arizona	132,782	8.7%	54,833
Arkansas	62,167	9.1%	30,111
California	953,557	10.3%	389,631
Colorado	70,555	6.4%	28,185
Connecticut	52,201	6.2%	21,123
Delaware	17,469	9.0%	7,803
Florida	345,134	9.5%	151,492
Georgia	218,208	10.1%	98,773
Hawaii	42,179	4.8%	13,814
Idaho	17,764	4.8%	7,087
Illinois	288,827	8.9%	119,676
Indiana	100,304	6.4%	39,180
Iowa	29,297	4.0%	11,230

State	Children in Kinship Care	% of states children	Grandparent Caregivers
Kansas	37,765	5.3%	16,184
Kentucky	69,435	6.9%	30,241
Louisiana	144,550	11.9%	64,866
Maine	11,354	3.8%	4,326
Maryland	129,487	9.6%	54,323
Massachusetts	87,502	5.8%	30,615
Michigan	183,621	7.0%	71,200
Minnesota	47,983	3.7%	19,053
Mississippi	101,556	13.1%	46,693
Missouri	96,412	6.8%	39,188
Montana	11,907	4.2%	5,161
Nebraska	18,621	4.2%	8,321
Nevada	44,898	8.8%	19,278
New Hampshire	12,458	4.1%	3,869
New Jersey	171,395	8.2%	63,514
New Mexico	51,657	10.2%	21,279
New York	409,045	12.6%	165,493
North Carolina	174,201	7.1%	80,126
North Dakota	4,980	3.1%	2,414
Ohio	192,631	6.6%	76,794
Oklahoma	72,426	8.2%	34,185
Oregon	51,617	6.1%	20,735
Pennsylvania	201,853	6.9%	76,356
Rhode Island	14,603	5.9%	5,170
South Carolina	112,044	11.2%	49,894
South Dakota	10,716	5.3%	5,146
Tennessee	126,284	9.1%	56,682
Texas	601,820	10.2%	244,100
Utah	41,916	5.7%	13,756
Vermont	5,033	3.5%	1,838
Virginia	138,678	8.0%	56,663
Washington	85,991	5.7%	35,761
West Virginia	28,216	7.0%	10,809
Wisconsin	61,165	4.5%	25,373
Wyoming	6,379	5.0%	2,738
District of Columbia	22,097	16.4%	10,702